LIGHTS,
CAMERA,
PASSION!

Discover Passion. Discover Happiness. Discover Success.

Tales from a TV studio and other walks of life

Award-winning TV personality

DARIN ADAMS

Lights, Camera, Passion

Book design by Rebecca Hayes, http://beckypublisher.com

Cover art and design by Chad Lanenga

Published in the United States by
Sage Lane Media
Fruit Heights, UT 80437

ISBN-13: 978-0-9896585-0-8

Library of Congress Control Number 2013911976

To my parents.
They taught me their passions, they exposed
me to what they loved, they helped me see
the joy that comes from pursuing joy.

Now that I'm grown, I've discovered their
greatest passion was simply my happiness.

Acknowledgments

I've never been one to let details stand in the way of a good story. While I have done my best to make sure I have all the details correct in these stories, I'll be the first to admit, they might not pass the test of a Smithsonian Institute authenticator. With that in mind, I must thank the many people who allowed me to share their stories. They shared their time, insight, and experiences for the benefit of the rest of us.

Mentors like Ty Bennett, Doug Nielsen, and Jason Hewlett were the first to ask, "Have you written your book?" long before it was even conceived.

Becky Hayes shared her expertise and Chad Lanenga shared his artistic insight to make mere words come alive.

My parents, LaVere and Karelyn Adams spent countless hours reading, revising, correcting, and advising. It's one of the great advantages of having phenomenal parents who just so happen to be really smart schoolteachers.

My children, Parker, "Norm", Brooklyn, and Baxter have been putting up with my talk of passions throughout this whole process and deserve special thanks for humoring me, and supporting me. And my wonderful wife, Kristi, has been my rock through it all, encouraging me and supporting my passions.

Sincere thanks to you all.

Contents

1

Baby Showers & Turtlenecks

It all comes down to Passion

"Baby Showers!" came the cry from Brooke as she burst into the office and headed for our cluster of cubicles. "I have found the perfect person for baby showers."

I was working as a host of a daily, lifestyle TV program. We were constantly in search of interesting topics and interesting people who could address them. "Interesting," so I discovered, is a relative term.

While I never gave baby showers a second thought, except to be clear of the house if one were being thrown, baby showers seemed to fit the definition of "interesting" to the rest of my all-female co-workers.

The party planner my co-host Brooke had stumbled across had strong feelings about baby showers. (I had strong views, too. But no one cared about those.) This woman felt that baby showers had gotten out of hand. A woman should have one baby shower. It should be with her close friends. It should be an opportunity to talk and visit. Now to me, those didn't seem like radical ideas. But for women who spent their afternoons at showers identifying melted candy bars in Pampers diapers, putting diapers on baby dolls while blindfolded, or dangling a threaded needle over the pregnant mother's hand to determine the gender, those ideas were radical. They were downright revolutionary.

It could mean the end to shower foods as we know them. No more ribbon sandwiches with egg salad, or frothy fruity punch with enough carbonation to float the Titanic. Nut cups and little glass food trays might be taking a back seat. For women who attend and throw dozens of showers, this was the kind of "Baby Shower Bible" information they were dying to hear.

So this woman, with all her ideas and opinions and notions was invited to come on the show. It was bound to be edge-of-your-seat scintillating.

On that same show, our fashion expert Holly Stone was also invited to come on. (Now in all reality, I don't think it was really the exact same show. But for sake of literary license, let's just pretend it was the same show. It's not going to affect the outcome of the story. And it just makes it easier to tell. So bear with me.)

Holly was doing a segment on some fashion trend. It might have been knee-high boots with military buckles. It might have been brightly patterned leggings that make your legs look like oversized bumblebees. It might have been belt buckles as big as pizza stones. Knowing Holly and her flair for pulling off fashion, it could have been all three. But we had also asked Holly to come up with her "favorite fashion find." A make-up product. A hair clip. A piece of funky jewelry. While she was out and about, surely she had seen some "must have" item that she would want to share with us.

That "find" was revealed to us ahead of time in a planning meeting. It was a turtleneck.

A turtleneck! Surely there had to have been something more compelling and interesting than a turtleneck. We were heading into spring and the only people thinking about turtlenecks were, well, turtles. Did she need more time to find something else? Did we need to suggest something else that would be flashier and more interesting? Should we just go ahead and let her tout her turtleneck?

Holly, we were told, was committed to the turtlenecks. So we held our breath, gave it the okay, and trepiditiously moved forward.

And so, on the day under scrutiny, the program began. The opening of the show rolled. Right off the top of the show, we hyped the fact that we had the authoritative word on baby showers. A display had been set up and it, along with the accompanying narration, was the first thing viewers saw. We promised examples of baby showers that would transform how you think about them. There were color coordinated decorations and invitations and banners and bunting. It was baby showers as we had never done them before. They were coming up in just ten minutes.

And then there were the turtlenecks. Mentions of them: not so much. That segment was buried in the show and was given about a third of the time budgeted for baby showers. It wasn't teased or promoted. Anyone tuning in for information on turtlenecks that day wouldn't have been given a hint that they were even on. (Not that we get many people tuning in for information on turtlenecks.)

We began moving along through the segments outlined as part of that day's show.

The interview with the party planner/baby shower expert was conducted by my co-host Brooke. It didn't seem right that a man would be doing the segment. (My yawning or dozing off in the middle of it might have seemed rude.)

Now, I don't want to embarrass this wonderful, creative woman who spent countless hours getting ready for her TV appearance. So, for the sake of this story, we'll just call her Barbara Jackson. That's not her real name, so don't go wondering if every Barbara Jackson you have ever met is the one I'm talking about.

With a wonderful blend of enthusiasm and professionalism, my co-host Brooke introduced Barbara Jackson as the woman behind the ideas that would revolutionize baby showers. She set up the concept and tossed a question to Barbara regarding "open house" showers where guests show up whenever they want. It's an easy enough topic since it's Barbara's big pet peeve.

Screeech! Stop the show right there. Before we go another second into the show, let me set the stage inside a TV studio.

There are dozens of bright lights pointed at you. Each one feels like 1/12th the power of the sun. There are giant cameras pointed at you like some laser-equipped weapons from Star Wars. There are studio crew members walking about, readying other parts of the set for future segments, oblivious to you and your nerves.

Let me also set the stage for what's going on inside the minds of most of our guests. They likely didn't sleep well the night before, or the night before that. They have rehearsed in their mind a thousand times what they're going to say. They have spent hours worrying about critically important details, like if their outfit matches or what earrings to wear or how to wear their hair – weighty stuff there. Their heart might be pounding. Their hands might be sweating. Their knees might be knocking.

Picture that, and then a host turning to you and asking you a question, expecting you to be intelligent and composed and authoritative.

For all of Barbara's intentions and preparations and opinions, the pounding, sweating and knocking got the better of her.

She started out well enough. But the words didn't seem to come quickly... anything but. Her speech pattern started getting slower and slower. And then it literally stopped. She was in mid-sentence.

"As moms... want... to..."

There was an audible pause.

It only lasted three of four seconds. But it seemed like an eternity. This is TV. We talk on TV.

It wasn't the end of the world, but it felt like it for a moment.

Brooke, always at the ready, jump-started the conversation again, and the segment went forward, showcasing some of Barbara's creative ideas for staging a shower. Barbara is an amazing event planner with enough inspiration to throw a thousand showers. But somehow, in that three-second pause and the few seconds leading up to it, some of that brilliance got lost.

It was harder to recall the suggestions for a themed party than it was to recall the silent three-second pause.

The show felt like it was in a tailspin and as we looked at the rundown, the next segment wasn't about to help pull us out of it.

Up next was the segment we had tried to tuck somewhere unnoticed into the lineup.

We were going from bad to worse. Up next: turtlenecks.

After our less than stirring foray into baby showers, we could feel the proverbial wheels coming off the track on the show. We certainly weren't planning on submitting the show for any award competitions. This one couldn't get over soon enough.

Brooke and I introduced the idea that in all of Holly's adventures, she was bound to discover some new little hidden gem. We wanted Holly to share her discovery with us, and we had invited her to fill us in on exactly what her breakthrough "favorite find" was. We knew that turtlenecks were hardly a breakthrough discovery or a hidden gem. So it was with a little hesitation that we turned to Holly and asked, "So Holly, what is your favorite fashion find?"

That's when the lights came on. They came on in Holly's face. She was literally on the edge of her seat and leaned forward even more as she gushed, "Turtlenecks!" She held up these turtlenecks and let us feel them. They looked like plain cotton, but as she described the wonderful, lightweight fabric, it almost seemed that we were handling some exotic magical cloth woven on some magical loom from the Orient. She pulled out a dizzying array of colors that, with her vision, would add the perfect dash of color to any outfit. She conjured up every possible wardrobe need and with her intoxicating vision, showed how adding that simple turtleneck would be the answer to making any outfit absolutely perfect.

And then, after she had drawn us into her euphoria, she lowered her voice and leaned back just a bit. It was enough to make us lean forward. "And the best part of all?" she queried with a twinkle and a wry smile.

How could it get any better? She already had us whipped into a frenzy with the fabric, colors, and practical uses of this seemingly magical garment.

She leaned back into us and after a fraction of a pause, she burst out, "It's only $1.72!"

Jaws dropped. Hearts quickened. Breaths gasped.

"They were already on sale and then this week, they were put on clearance in addition to that," she gushed on. "It's a special deal at Old Navy and I just checked and they still have plenty of colors. They have a great selection. I love these turtlenecks and they are my favorite fashion find!"

She could have recited the Preamble to the Constitution after that. It didn't matter what else she said. She had succeeded in getting everyone watching excited about something as simple as a turtleneck. A shirt. A piece of fabric. Something that was really nothing more than some cloth had somehow taken on near magical qualities and everyone now had to have it.

As soon as the show was over, we had emails and calls. We had other employees in the building coming back to the studio to ask exactly where that turtleneck could be found. Of course, no one was around to answer the calls, questions or emails. As soon as the show was over, half our staff had made a beeline across the street to the nearest Old Navy before the selection of turtlenecks was picked over.

And that's when, after 25 years of being in TV, it hit me. It came down to one word: Passion.

I have interviewed countless people on TV. Some are celebrities. Some are business owners. Some are PR professionals. Some are stay at home moms. Some of them make phenomenal TV. Some of them make forgettable TV. It doesn't matter how much money they make. It doesn't matter how successful they are. It doesn't matter how many times they have been on TV.

What matters, is passion.

I frequently have to "prep" guests to appear on TV. These are people who have likely never appeared on TV. They're about to go on-air to talk about something they know a lot about. It could be furnace systems. It could be garden plants. It could be painting or penguins or push pins. These people are likely experts in their fields. That's why we have them on TV. There are several things we tell them.

DARIN-ISM NO. 1

Passion is the vehicle to get thoughts and ideas engaged with our soul.

First, don't ever look at the camera. There are three cameras in the studio, and if a guest tries to look at the camera, chances are, it will be the wrong camera. I was doing a cooking segment in the kitchen with a professional chef. Two of the cameras were zeroed in on us showing the techniques and the ingredients. One of the cameras was a "hand held" camera. A mobile cameraman would use that camera to occasionally get in close for some tight shots of the food. The chef spotted that camera and was sure it was the only one being used. It was off to the side of the set and was clearly not being used. But the chef turned his whole body toward it. The hand held camera wasn't on a tripod and was being held down lower. So the chef leaned over holding food toward it. The whole time, the other cameras straight in front of the kitchen were the ones being used. Viewers at home sat there watching the strangest cooking segment I can remember, where the chef was turned sideways, flashing only a profile, and bending over talking to what appeared to some imaginary gnome off to the side of the kitchen. Remember, don't try to look at the camera.

We also tell guests not to wear some patterns or colors. Small houndstooth patterns are a no-no. The camera has a hard time distinguishing the patterns and it ends up creating a moiré look. A guest ends up looking like a rainbow trout with shining, luminescent multi-colored rays emanating from their clothing. It ends up looking like a fabric version of the northern lights. We also tell guests to wear rich colors. Often, we seat a guest on a black couch for an interview. There are always those who think that black is slimming. On TV, it can be slimming in a bad way.

They disappear into the color of the couch and seem to vanish. It looks like a floating head bobbing around. That could be good if it were a Halloween show and we wanted to make it look like a levitating head. But for a guest prepared to talk about something important to them, the decapitated head isn't a good look.

The most important thing we tell someone is that there is no substitution for passion. Passion comes across like nobody's business. People can feel your commitment and enthusiasm and energy. Someone could forget all of their talking points. They could mix up words. They could be nothing more than a floating head, rainbow trout gnome-befriending profile and it wouldn't matter. People feel passion.

Passion is the vehicle to get thoughts and ideas engaged with our soul.

Passion is life. Passion is success. Passion is power. Passion is control.

Because we see it on camera day after day, we tell one mantra to our guests more than any other. It all comes down to passion. There is no substitution for passion.

2

In Quest of Toaster Strudels

What is Passion?

People can think of different things when you mention the word passion. If you think of love or a strong, *and I mean* **strong** *desire*, then your mind is wandering where it shouldn't.

People hear that phrase of someone being in the "throes of passion." What in the world is that? I mean, have you ever used the word "throes" in your life. "Throes" isn't a noun like that. Throws is a verb. The boy throws a ball. I guess a throw is also one of those little blankets that you toss over a sofa or chair for decorative purposes. And maybe someone has some of those they use for passionate things. So I guess if you're caught up in the moment and you have a couple of those throws wrapped around you and your beloved, then that would be a case of being in the "throws of passion." And now your mind is *really* wandering where it shouldn't.

So if that's not the kind of passion we want to explore, then what is?

Definitions of passion often involve words like powerful, compelling, emotional, enthusiastic or intense.

Those are strong words and are reserved for a strong feeling. Passion is not a passing feeling. It goes much deeper.

There are three types of things that you might do. Things you do. Things you do well. And things you do with passion. Don't get confused.

Things We Do:

There are things that we all do every day. We might not enjoy doing them. We might not do them very well. But we still do them.

I wake up. I drive to work. I eat a cookie for breakfast. I wash it down with a glass of Metamucil. I get tired at my computer and pretend to be meditating when I'm really sleeping. I eat another cookie. I drink lots of water. I check my email 50 times a day.

I simply do these things. They give me very little pleasure. None of them really gets me going (aside from the Metamucil). I'm not really much better for doing these things.

Unfortunately, for many of us, most of our day is filled with doing these things. Things we have to do. Things we have gotten used to doing. Things we "just plain do."

Things We Do Well:

Then there are things we do well. We might have a special talent or gift or ability.

I'm not a great soccer player. When I was young, other teams were the Dragons or the Tigers or the Spitting Cobras (I learned the hard way to not get too close to the Spitting Cobras.) Our team was the Crickets. That should give you an indication of my skill level. But I'm trying to make up for it now as a dad. I have coached teams for all four of my kids.

I think I'm a pretty good soccer coach. I have found fun games to play for soccer practice. We don't run laps. We run while we play "Sharks and Minnows." We don't do precision kicking drills. We learn precision while playing "Pirates and Ships." We don't do endless ball control exercises. We learn those skills while playing "Traffic Cop." Everyone gets a nickname. I cheer wildly until I lose my voice. We have fun whether we win or lose. I'm not the winningest coach, but I still volunteer each year and always field a fun team. Here's my confession. I don't always enjoy it. When I'm coaching two teams, it eats up some time with practices during the week, and then games on Saturdays. When the first practice rolls around in the spring and fall, I am not always enthusiastic. And I sure do enjoy celebrating the final game of each season. I do it because I enjoy spending time with my kids, but I sometimes wouldn't mind if someone else were coaching.

Coaching soccer is something I do well, even though I don't always absolutely love everything about it.

At work, we have a small staff which produces an hour TV show each day. We each are assigned various segments to produce. That involves getting in touch with the guest or presenter and mapping out what we want to accomplish during the segment and how we want to do it. Some on our staff do a great job working with crafty projects. Others do well with fashion segments. And there are those who are great with empowering and educational topics. My boss likes to give me the newcomers. She thinks I do well with helping people who are coming on for the first time. They are often local business owners who are introducing a new product or concept to the market. They often have ideas of what they want to do with their time on TV. Those ideas are often wrong, very wrong. So it's my assignment to help them see how best to use their appearance.

My boss assigns me that because she seems to think that I do a good job with them. (She also thinks Diet Coke is a good option for a breakfast drink.) Just because she thinks I do a good job with them doesn't mean I enjoy doing it. There are some days I want to scream. There are some days that I do scream. My co-workers have seen more than one day when I have jumped up after talking to someone on the phone and bellowed. It's not a long bellow. It's just a quick one. It's a cross between a rutting elk and an angry sea cow. Then, having vented, I sit back down and get back to work.

It's not just something I do. It's something I do well. (I'm talking about producing the segments, not the bellowing.) But it doesn't mean it's my passion. I don't get excited about it. Simply because we do something well, does NOT make it a passion. If it doesn't make your heart skip a beat, if it doesn't give you a little charge, if it doesn't make you say, "Give it to me! I want that!" then it's not a passion.

Things We Do With Passion:

Then there comes the most exciting category. The cat's meow, the bee's knees and every other animal body part you want to throw in the mix.

These are things you do with passion. These are things that give you *butterflies in your stomach* just thinking about. They're the things you don't pass up an opportunity to do. They are the things that get you excited about just the possibility.

Think of a time when you felt exhilaration and pure joy. What were you doing? That's something you likely do with passion.

It was likely something small. It might have affected other people, but could also have been very personal. It doesn't have to affect large numbers. It only has to affect you.

The only way to do great work is to love what you do. If you haven't found it yet, keep looking. Don't settle. As with all matters of the heart, you'll know it when you find it.
- *Steve Jobs*

I was working at a TV station in Louisville, Kentucky as the morning feature reporter. That meant that I would add a little fun and personality to the morning news program. In between rehashing the old news from the night before, and repeating the traffic and weather reports every ten minutes, they would come to me at some interesting location. I might be flying off in a hot air balloon one day, and going under the knife for surgery the next day. It was a crazy adventure.

But one day, my General Manager called me in. He sensed that my job, while fun, might not be a long term solution. You don't see a lot of 60 year old men with jobs like that. He also sensed that my growing family would likely need more money than I was making. He would know. He had just cut my salary.

He sat there in a glass enclosed office, overlooking the busy street and the station's parking lot. That's when he asked me if I had ever considered a job in TV Sales. These are the guys who sell the advertisements that appear on TV.

Now the thought of sales didn't immediately appeal to me. It seemed sleazy. So I said, "Bill, it seems sleazy." I didn't try hard to couch my words.

"When I think of sales," I continued, "I picture some used car salesman with a loud jacket trying to force someone to buy something they don't want to buy. I picture them being self-centered and pushy."

"You do remember," he said peering over the top of his glasses, "that I was in TV Sales for about 20 years, don't you?"

I had unfortunately forgotten that fact.

He pointed out someone getting into a car in the parking lot below. It was a dark, shiny car with options that I never knew existed. "That person," Bill casually tossed out," makes well into the six digits. They're in sales. And they're not even our best seller. The top money maker in this building isn't anyone in management. And it's not one of our high priced anchors. It's a salesperson. Sales is where the money is."

With that lucrative incentive, I began to rethink my hasty decision. "Well, when you put it that way...." I started in, "I guess I could do sales."

That was my fatal flaw, and partly the reason I'm not in sales today.

"But you can't have that kind of attitude or it's never going to work," Bill changed his tone. His rah-rah cheerleader turned into a wise Master Shifu from Kung Fu Panda. "What makes a person successful in sales is all in the attitude. They have a different kind of mentality. When they're in a meeting, they can hardly wait to get out and start selling. When they get an idea or a lead, they're just thinking, 'Give it to me, let me go, I want this more than anything.' That's what makes them successful. That's what it takes. If you've got that, you'll be great. If you don't have it, it will feel sleazy to you."

He was talking passion. He was basically asking if I had the passion to make it work. He needed someone who got tingly about the thought of helping businesses get exposure through TV.

I sat there looking at him. I glanced longingly down at the shiny, black car which was now streaking down the street. I wanted to say yes to fancy lunch meetings. I wanted to say yes to designer suits. I wanted to say yes to burled walnut interior trim, Dolby surround sound and heated lumbar massage seats. But we were talking passion here, and frankly, I didn't have the passion that he was looking for.

DARIN-ISM NO. 2

Passions don't have to affect large numbers. They just have to affect you.

I had passion for lots of other things.

I had been working at a TV station in Pocatello, Idaho. I was the evening weatherman. For years, it had been a dream job where I didn't have long hours, a lengthy commute or any heavy lifting. I even got to spend some of my summer morning hours working with a friend who was a landscaper. I got to get my hands dirty and be creative at the same time.

After more than 8 years of working there, I was surprised to hear that the station had been sold. The new owners were some big corporation from the big city. They came in with their big plans and big changes. The new TV campaign was "Change is Good." But I knew better. While the changes turned out to be better for me in the long run, they were still a blow.

They started a morning news program and moved me from my "cush" evening gig to waking up at 4:00 a.m. to report weather. The management had basically told me to tone down my on-air presentation. They told me not to talk quickly, not to move my arms around too much while talking weather, not to make jokes, not to move much…not to be *me*. And as long as I could conform, I didn't need to worry about losing my job.

It didn't take much to realize that they didn't want me. I was quickly beaten into submission.

Since it was getting close to summer, I still enjoyed dabbling a bit from time to time with my landscaping friend, Rick. One day he shared an idea he had. He thought I should make a mossy millstone fountain in my backyard.

The next day, I showed up bleary-eyed for work as usual. Amy Westerby was the cute, perky blonde who did the hourly morning news updates. Every station has to have one of those. "Amy," I blurted out when I saw her coming into the studio getting ready. "I have to tell you about what I want to do. I want to make a mossy millstone fountain!"

From her reaction, I could tell that she clearly didn't have a clue what a mossy millstone fountain was. So I elaborated. "You take some Spanish moss and some peat moss and any kind of moss you can find. Then you mix it in with some concrete and pour it into a mold. This would be a flat circle, like a millstone shape. That's why they call it a mossy millstone." I ran through the directions as if someone should know what a mossy millstone was, when in reality, Rick and I had only conjured up the idea the day before. "It lays flat but you have water pumped up underneath it and the water bubbles up out of the hole in the middle of the millstone. Then it trickles over the side and down a little stream, until it collects, and then gets pumped back up through the hole in the millstone again. I want to put it in my backyard right by the deck," I continued on while Amy took it all in.

She really wasn't listening to my directions. Instead, she was just watching my reactions. Finally, when I was done, she proclaimed, "You have to do it!"

Eager for her endorsement, I asked, "Don't you think it will be cool?"

"I have no idea, and I don't know if I really even understand it. But you have to do it because this is the most excited I have seen you about anything since I have known you."

Sure, she had only known me less than a year. But still, it was a pronouncement that hit me square in the face. It was clearly the most excited I had been. I had fallen into a rut at work. I had grown depressed about my employment situation and felt I had little to look forward to. I had become mundane. And then, along came my little mossy millstone. It had lit me up. It had given me drive and excitement. It had given me passion.

For months, I had been living without passion. For whatever reason, grounded or not, I had turned over anything that I had passion about to some time in the future. Amy and the mossy millstone helped me see what I had been missing, and made me realize how exciting, exhilarating and life-altering a little passion can be.

You gotta stop wearing your wishbone where your backbone oughta be.
~ Richard from Texas
Eat, Pray, Love by Elizabeth Gilbert

Just like a sales person who has the passion and can hardly wait to get at that next contact, I too, would have felt, "Give me that moss, I'm making me a millstone."

When a high school offers to give tours of their facility, normally, it's not a big deal. But the high school down the street from the TV station was no ordinary high school. It was East High School, the same campus where the "High School Musical" franchise was shot. We chatted it up on the air about the prospect of taking a tour and seeing the gym and cafeteria and places that had been immortalized in the Disney "made-for-TV" musical. The real-life East High theater department was putting on the stage version of the fictionalized East High's "High School Musical." We interviewed the local high school actors playing Troy and Gabriella who revealed that they had ticket requests from people around the country, and even overseas, who were converging on the real East High for the production. It was like a pilgrimage to some holy shrine, and hundreds of devout followers were making the trek.

High School Musical is a fun show that has been described as a modern-day "Romeo and Juliet." Troy Bolton is the star basketball player who is convinced to try out for the high school musical. Gabriella Montez is the intellectually gifted bookworm who is persuaded to do the same thing. They come from different backgrounds and shouldn't be associating together. Thus, the Romeo and Juliet comparison.

Instead, I like to think that it's a show about passions.

Sure, there are the obvious passions. These two high school students are smitten, madly in love. They also have their talents of basketball for Troy and academics for Gabriella. They still find a way to pursue those, and magically try out for the high school musical. Gotta love Disney and those happy endings.

But a couple of my favorite characters aren't even listed on the back of the DVD cases.

One of Troy's basketball teammates was Zeke Baylor. And just as Troy really got a thrill from being onstage with Gabriella (or being anywhere with Gabriella) Zeke had a secret passion. It was baking. "I love to bake!" he finally gets up the courage to boldly proclaim. "Strudels, scones, even apple pandowdy." I don't even know what an apple pandowdy is, but I can feel his excitement for it. For years, he had felt the peer pressure to keep his passion under wraps and just focus on what he does best: put the ball in the hoop. But with his passion unleashed and out in the open, he shows off his crème brulee, and later unveils his cake baked in the shape of the mathematical symbol for pi. It's a good luck gift to Gabriella and her scholastic decathlon teammate Taylor on the day of their big match. He even uses his passion to whip up some cookies for Sharpay, his secret crush (there's that other kind of passion again).

And Martha Cox is the super-smart brainiac who has never revealed her true passion. But there's something about the whole student body prancing around the school cafeteria at lunch time, confessing their deep dark passions. It's contagious. And Martha jumps up to proudly shout, "I love to pop and lock and jam and break." (That's dancing for those of you who can't decipher that gibberish.) "Sometimes I think it's more fun than homework!" (Remember she's the studious type.) Even though others around her try to persuade her to stick to what she does best, acing scholastic tests, she knows her inner passion of break dancing is anxious to break out.

By the second movie, Martha is dancing more and more with the rest of the crowd as they look to her as the primo pop and locker. Zeke, meanwhile, is whipping up concoctions in the kitchen at the country club where the entire student body has somehow been employed for the summer. (The student employees at Lava Springs Country Club seem to outnumber the guests by about 7 to 1.)

By the time the trilogy of the High School Musical franchise wrapped up, Zeke and Martha were more synonymous with their recently revealed passions, i.e.: cooking and break dancing, than with their original props of basketballs and brains. Under a blazingly blue sky, and flanked by mountains in the distance, the graduating class gathered for their commencement. Troy delivered the show's parting message with a gospel-esque choir swaying back and forth and a full symphony backing him up.

"East High is a place where teachers encouraged us to break the status quo and define ourselves as we choose," he affirmed proudly. "Where a jock can cook up a mean crème brulee." The camera cut to Zeke smiling broadly as his schoolmates cheered him on. "And a brainiac can break down on a dance floor." Cut to Martha who jumped to her feet while busting a move. He then went on to blather some gobbledygook about some girl-stuff. But the real message had just been made.

And with that, the entire student body did what they had done on the golf course, in the school cafeteria and on the basketball court. They spontaneously broke out in song and dance. Cheering and pumping their fists in the air, they instinctively created formations and executed intricately choreographed moves. And front and center, well, almost front and center, but just a little behind the Troy and Gabriella characters, was Martha. The girl who shed her studious title to wade into the break dancing role was grabbing the spotlight because she had grabbed her passion. As a side note, Zeke was also in the final number, but was edged out slowly as the number wore on. My personal theory is that he was gradually sneaking out so he could race home and whip up a batch of cookies to celebrate.

The woman who follows the crowd will usually go no further than the crowd. The woman who walks alone is likely to find herself in places no one has ever been before.

~ *Albert Einstein*

I have another area where I have a passion. It's a little odder, and I'm a little embarrassed about it. But I'm just going to get it off my chest. I have a passion for finding a bargain.

Every Sunday morning, one of the first things I do is grab the Sunday paper. I begin looking forward to it on Saturday. I grab the inserted ads and discard the rest of the paper for anyone else in the family who actually wants to read the news, check the scores or browse the funnies. Armed with a 3x5 card and a pen, I go through the flyers from the various stores and jot down the items that are great deals. The card goes up on the fridge so that anyone who is heading to those stores can pick up the great bargains.

You can imagine that not many other people are impressed with my drive for finding bargains (including my wife). They're fine if they save some money here or there, but most people don't have that passion to race out for the newspaper, just to rip open the ads. For me, it's passion that gets me out of bed on Sunday morning.

One wintry Sunday morning, I popped open the ad for Meijer, a "big box" grocery store in the upper Midwest. On the front page, I noticed bigger than normal print on the ad. That shot a little extra adrenalin into my system. They were offering a deal where, if you bought five items, they would give you a coupon for five dollars off of a future purchase. Whatever it is in your body that makes adrenalin was cranking right then. And then, I spotted the real clincher. Some of the items that were part of the promotion were actually on sale for less than a dollar each. Adrenalin overload!

For those of you who might be mathematically challenged, let me do a quick math lesson here. If you buy five items for less than five dollars, and then the store gives you five dollars back, you are earning money and getting free food. I had been excited before about deals that *saved* me money. But I had never found one that would actually *pay* me money.

I ran to my wife and shared my excitement. "That's nice, dear," she said while she was ironing our daughter's dress for church. "Could you hand me that spray bottle?"

I ran to my young son, and tried to explain the promotion to him. "Does it include Pokemon cards?" was his response.

I resorted to tracking down our 1-year old who at least appeared to be listening to me while I mapped out my plan of attack for the week.

The execution of that plan began the next day. I stopped by the store on my way home from work. I picked up five cake mixes, took them confidently to the check out line. I scanned them and the total came up to $3.90. I swiped my card and as I did, some machine printed out a coupon for five dollars off my next purchase. My eyes sparkled.

I ran my bags out to the car and dashed right back in. I picked up five more cake mixes, hurried up to the front and this time, I paid with my coupon. But this time, the cashier gave me a dollar and change back, and the machine spat out another five dollar coupon. I was nearing giddiness as I threw the sacks in the back seat of my car and headed right back in again. Frozen vegetables were also a sub-dollar item. So on my next trip through, I grabbed five bags of those along with five cake mixes. Two more coupons and more change awaited me at the checkout line.

As I glanced at the circular one more time, scanning it to find what other items were part of the promotion, my eyes stopped dead in their tracks. There it was. Toaster Strudel. It almost seemed too good to be true. Toaster Strudels were a rarity at our house. We had them only on special occasions. They were a bit pricey for our budget. But that all changed on that Monday afternoon. Toaster Strudel was finally approachable.

They would end up being a little more than a dollar, but if I carefully balanced out my purchases with the sub-dollar cake mixes to offset them, I could still walk away spending practically nothing.

I planned my attack and wrangled enough Toaster Strudel boxes to pack the freezer. I started feeling numb. It was either from the sheer bliss or the frozen Toaster Strudel boxes.

Eventually, I finally decided to call it quits for the day. It might have had something to do with my overflowing back car seat.

I burst through the door at home holding as many bags as my arms could carry. "Guess how much this cost!" I exclaimed to my wife who had one of those doubtful looks on her face. "I don't know, tell me."

"No, really," I repeated. "Guess how much it cost me." I was a little more forceful.

"Really, I don't know," she repeated. "just tell me."

"GUESS HOW MUCH IT COST ME!" I was embarrassingly agitated at this point.

She sensed my persuasion, spun around from wiping off the counter and with her hand on her hip, she eyed the sacks. "Okay, 20 bucks," she guessed, knowing that I obviously had gotten a killer deal or I wouldn't have been yelling for her response.

"Nothing!" I gushed. "It didn't cost me a dime. It was all free. IT WAS FREE! And I got change back!" My arms were laden down with the grocery sacks, but I still wanted her to get the full effect of just how much money I had made. So I stuck out my leg with the pocket containing all the change and bills, and hopped up and down on the other leg, hoping the jangling of the loose coins and the sight of the bulging wad of bills would be enough to impress her.

Try as she might, she couldn't ignore my accomplishment. "You just went in and bought all that and you got that?" she asked, gesturing to the sacks and then the money.

"Yeah," I was still euphoric at the explanation. "It was just like they were paying me money to take food out."

She was now a little more intrigued. "I can't believe you got all that by going through the checkout line in one quick trip."

"Well," I admitted a little sheepishly, "it wasn't just one quick trip."

"How many times did you have to go through," her detective skills kicked in.

"Eight or nine or ten," my voice got trailed off a bit as I had to admit the lengths to which I had gone. "And then I had to take the food out to the car between each purchase, but yeah. It was that simple!"

That's when the bubble burst for her. "I can't believe you actually went through the line that many times. I would never do that," she sighed as she eyed the 25 cake mixes I had just hauled in the door. Of course she wouldn't. It wasn't her passion.

That week, I told at least a dozen other friends about my discovery. But while they were intrigued about the chance to earn money by taking home cake mixes, frozen vegetables and other food products, none of them actually put it into practice. It wasn't the passion of any of them either.

But it was mine, and every other time I went to the store that week and stocked up on the aforementioned items, plus even more extravagant items like cookie mixes, muffin mixes and as many Toaster Strudels as I could carry, I smiled inside. Each time I got one of those five dollar coupons, I got excited. I thrilled at the thought of the phenomenal deal I was getting. Sure, there were snags at times; I had to go to Customer Service when the coupon didn't appear on demand. I had to debate with a cashier whether or not I could spend a coupon to get another coupon. But I emerged triumphant at the end of the week with a freezer stocked full of food, and shelves in the basement packed with more baked good products than Betty Crocker could imagine. And inside, I felt giddy and warm.

That feeling wasn't from the Boston Cream Pie Toaster Strudel.

It was from feeding my passion.

3

How Can You Mess Up Film Chain?

Passions change!

TV was not my first love. In fact it wasn't even near the top of the list. TV trailed somewhere behind Pop Rocks and only slightly ahead of a tetanus shot. It was mostly because I hadn't really considered TV as a profession.

When I went to college, I was planning to major in some other communications-related field like advertising or public relations. But when I enrolled in classes in the communications field, I started running into other students who had visions of TV news in their starry eyes.

As it turned out, there was a college-run TV news broadcast that took place every evening. Some of my new "newsie" friends were on the volunteer list and they headed down to the studio each evening to help out. "C'mon and do it with us," they coaxed me one afternoon as we left our speech class. "It's better than just sitting around your dorm room staring at cinder blocks."

With that ringing endorsement, I tagged along. The studio was a big cavernous room filled with lights, cameras, and action. There were people bustling around, preparing scripts and readying the set. There were some obviously older students who appeared to take themselves very seriously. They had to be the on-air students. They were pacing the floor and reading over scripts. There were others hurrying in and out of the control room, the nerve center of the operation where orders are barked over headsets to cameramen and support staff. At first blush, I was mesmerized. As I watched the proceedings of that first newscast, I became captivated. I had been bitten by the bug. Sign me up.

I became a volunteer for the broadcast and showed up every time they would take me. There was a large dry erase board in the newsroom with a person's assignment written on it. I was always excited whenever I spotted my name with a correlating task. There were all sorts of jobs to ensure that those exploring the TV news career path could get a good feel for what they wanted to do.

One of my first jobs was what was then called "film chain." When a news anchor is reading a story about some house fire, you'll see some picture of flames licking up the side of a house above the anchor's shoulder. Or if there's been a murder, there will be a photo of some chalk outline of a body. And if there's a marshmallow shortage, there will be a picture of an empty bag of Jet-Puffed marshmallows.

The "film chain" method is now completely archaic, but "back in the days," there was a large collection of slides. Each slide was for a different topic of stories likely to be used in a typical newscast. There was the "fire" slide, and the "murder" slide. There wasn't really a "marshmallow shortage" slide, as far as I can remember. That would be a specialty slide that would have to be created for a special occasion.

So, I would get a copy of the rundown of stories in the newscast and then go to the slide collection. I would pick out the correlating slides and put them in order. Then I would ascend a rickety spiral flight of metal stairs to a small, cramped closet-sized room that had the film chain machine. It resembled a large metal cabinet with two rotating slide wheels on the top. I would put the slides in order, alternating between the left wheel and the right wheel. Once I had all the slides loaded into the machine, all I had to do was stand there and push a button to advance the slide to the next picture. I just had to listen on a set of headphones to the director who would simply say to advance the slide. Listen, push the button. Listen, push the button. How could anything go wrong?

We were part-way through the newscast, and so far my listening and button pushing had been flawless. I was considering a job as a professional film chain operator. Then, with the push of a button, those dreams were dashed. There was a story about former first lady Betty Ford, for which I had loaded a slide of Mrs. Ford. The only problem was that I had loaded the slide in upside down.

As Mrs. Ford appeared behind the anchor, I heard gasps from the Control Room. There she hung upside down from the top of the TV screen like some bat bedding down for the night. The difference was that she was a former First Lady and appeared to be whispering in the anchor's ear. Then the gasps turned to shouts.

"The slide is upside down! Who put the slide in upside down? Lose the slide! Who is in Film Chain?! Who is in Film Chain?!" The shouts were getting more anxious.

"I am," I replied a bit timidly into my headset microphone.

"Who is in Film Chain?" came the reply. "Does anyone know who is in Film Chain?"

"I am. I'm here." This time it was a bit more confident.

"Is anyone in Film Chain? Someone go see what's happening in Film Chain!" The director was dispatching someone to check on me. I had to head them off.

"I'm here. I'm okay. I just loaded the slide in upside down," I pleaded back into the microphone. "I'll fix it. I'll just flip the slide around."

And with that, I reached my fingers into where the slide was loaded and tried to pull it out. What seemed like a great solution in my mind had two fatal flaws. First, the person who was supposed to "lose the slide" or remove the effect of the hanging First Lady hadn't done so. So she had been dangling there upside down for the entire reading of the story. And second, the film chain wasn't just taking some electronic image or anything like that. It was actually shooting light through the slide and capturing that image live. So as my fingers reached in to grab the slide, those fingers were also projected on the image behind the anchor.

What had been a bad enough situation with the inverted Betty Ford turned even worse as two giant oversized fingers reached in to grab her and pull her out. Viewers at home must have watched in horror as the anchor sat there reading the serious news report oblivious to the fact that it appeared some Godzilla-like monster was attacking Betty Ford and dragging her out of the scene.

It was about then that some fellow volunteer arrived on the scene after climbing up the stairs to check on me. I explained that I had been talking back to the director about what I was going to do. He patiently told me that I actually had to depress the red button to talk to anyone, a little detail that no one had managed to tell me about. He then climbed back down, having set me straight about what to never do during a newscast. (That would have been to never touch a slide for any reason.)

After the newscast, I should have been embarrassed. I should have crept out the back door when no one was watching. I should have wanted to never show my face there again.

Instead it was quite the opposite. I was exhilarated. This was my new-found passion. I loved the excitement and the thrill of being part of a live TV newscast. Who cares if everyone realized I didn't know how to work the headset intercom? Who cares if I had loaded the First Lady upside down? Who cares if those gigantic fingers grabbing at her were mine? That's a source of pride.

I could hardly wait for my next assignment. The faculty supervisor, in all his wisdom, decided to assign me to a different task. My next newscast found me working audio. I sat in another small room. There were a series of buttons and slider bars in front of me. When audio needed to come from somewhere, namely a pre-taped report or an anchor's mouth, it was my job to hit the button that fed that audio over the air, and adjust the slider bar to the preferred audio level. Seems simple enough. (But then again, so did the Film Chain.)

The opening sequence for the news began and I had the right button pushed for that audio. I was a little overwhelmed by the rush of excitement, and in that rush, forgot to push the buttons to click on the microphones for the two anchors. They started speaking. Of course, viewers at home didn't know that, since I hadn't pushed the buttons to activate their audio. It took several seconds for me to realize that. It was helped by the director who was shouting, "Audio, audio! Turn their mics on!" I think he shouted something similar to that about three times in a five-second time span. Boy, people can sure talk quickly and loudly when they get excited.

I punched up the right buttons and made it through the first block of the news with just a few other minor mistakes. I finally exhaled as I hit the buttons for the commercial break, glad I had made it through my first block of audio. My relief was short-lived.

"What is going on in audio?" came the anchor's voice over the airwaves. Little did they know, their conversation was now accidentally being broadcast over the commercial break.

"Some idiot is in there, I guess," quipped the other anchor. "How long did it take whoever it is to figure out our audio wasn't on for the top of the show? Hello! Hey, turn the mics on. We're talking out here," they laughed in their caustic and condescending way.

It didn't take me long to realize that I had now left their mics on. Of course, I was reminded by the director bellowing over the headset intercom, just in case that fact had escaped my attention. I didn't need the reminder. My fingers were frantically trying to find the right buttons to shut their audio off. I finally found the right button and clicked it off, much to the relief of viewers, other crew members, and of course, the two anchors, whose acerbic critique of my ability had just been broadcast to everyone watching.

Once again, by the time the newscast was over, I had long since forgotten any *faux pas* that might have occurred on my part. It had been another thrill for me. I was pushing buttons and making things happen. It was still my passion.

The third assignment I got on the newscast was operating the teleprompter. Teleprompters are now run digitally. It's done with computers and equipment I don't really understand. But back in those days, it was a lot more rudimentary.

The scripts were printed out via carbon copy paper. Then they were laid one by one on a small conveyor belt which was controlled by a small dial. Above the conveyor belt, a video camera was suspended, pointing down at the scripts rolling by. That signal was then run back out to the monitor mounted on the studio cameras the anchors were looking into while reading the stories.

Running the teleprompter consisted of placing the script pages one by one onto the conveyor belt. Then I would turn the dial to speed up or slow down the pace of the belt depending on the pace of the person reading. There was a small monitor in the cramped corner of the studio where the teleprompter was set up. It showed what the scripts looked like as they rolled by. There was even a thin red horizontal line toward the top. That was where, in a perfect world, the words would be as the anchor would be reading them.

Perfect worlds don't always exist.

I had seen other people run the teleprompter with skill and precision. They would carefully place the scripts on the belt and even pick them up at the other end of the conveyor belt after they had been read. They would stack them neatly in a pile. I figured this would be an easy task.

The anchors for the college broadcast rotated, giving more people a chance to get experience. It just so happened that the person assigned to read the news on my inaugural teleprompter run was the most energetic, high-octane student in the program. He always seemed as if he had just chugged a Red Bull. Of course, in those days, a Red Bull was a foreign term that could only refer to a college prank involving spray paint and nearby farm animals.

The energetic young man launched into his stories. His speed caught me off guard. I started trying to gauge his speed with the adjustable dial, but soon I realized that he was reading as fast as the dial would go. I cranked it all the way with my right hand. With my left hand, I grabbed the sheets of paper as quickly as I could and started slapping them down on the moving belt. My eyes were glued to the monitor, trying to keep the words close to the targeted red line. By the third page, I realized the words weren't on the red line. It was hard to describe exactly where they were. In my haste to place the pages on the belt, I hadn't noticed that I had been placing them outside the view of the suspended camera. I tried to straighten the pages, but in so doing, my arm was reaching across the lens of the camera blocking everything. I was working to straighten the pages with both hands which meant that my right hand was no longer twisting the dial to speed the belt along. In the few seconds it took for me to realize that, it dawned on me that I had now fallen behind where the anchor was reading.

The roadrunner of readers was now speeding along without me. He had given up on me and was now relying just on the stack of scripts he had on the set. I was determined to catch up. I tried to twist the dial as far as I could, and frantically kept grabbing the scripts and slapping them down. I never even attempted to pick them up at the other end of the belt. They piled up on the floor as I worked feverishly to get the words being read somewhere close to the red line. They never did.

Once again, I was not deterred. It had been a rush for me like none other. I was doing what I loved. It didn't matter that no one else loved me doing it. Fortunately, I was oblivious to the scowls of others. Thankfully, the debacle that had comprised my first few attempts at helping in broadcasting was overwhelmed in my mind by the thrill that had come from that same debacle.

It was my passion. It had driven me, not just through my college years, but for many years after that.

But passions change.

I still love TV. But it's not the same kind of passion as it was back then. In those early days, I would rather be at that TV studio than anywhere else on campus. It was where magic took place. It wasn't just the magic of broadcasting images through space to reappear on television sets. It was the magic of passion, the excitement and thrill that occurred when I was there. Even if I weren't scheduled to work a shift, I would go linger just to observe.

That kind of passion, for almost anything, is hard to maintain. But that's perfectly normal and healthy. We change as we go through life and acquire new experiences and incorporate them into our lives. And because of that, the things that thrill us and excite us will naturally change.

If gardening was a passion ten years ago, it's time for a reevaluation to see if it's still a passion. Years of weeding and planting might have taken a toll, and gardening may have tumbled from the top spot.

If reading historical drama used to get your heart racing, it may have lost some luster in your eyes. Do a quick check to see if you just think it's still the top spot, or if it indeed is your passion.

Do you still collect china dolls because you love the delicate figurines, or is it merely because your family *thinks* you love them and you can't bear to tell them you have moved on to something else?

Sometimes we outgrow our passions. Maybe we've fulfilled some challenge, and we need to progress. Sometimes a passion just isn't as age-appropriate as we mature and move on to other endeavors. Our lives change and our passions can certainly change with them. And sometimes dramatic life events can enter our life's plan, altering everything we think and know and force a change in priorities and passions.

Sometimes, on the way to the dream, you get lost and find a better one!
-Lisa Hammond

Amber Anderson was just months away from realizing her passion. She was on the fast track to become the next big thing in country music.

She had moved to Nashville eight years earlier and had done everything right. For five years, she had been working in the music industry. She was a studio musician. She was a demo artist. She wrote songs. She did lunch with Faith Hill. She was networking with all the right people and working with all the powerful ones.

After five years, she moved into the publishing office for the mega-group *Alabama*. She had her plan mapped out and continued getting closer and closer. The MCA record company had an opening on their label for a female singer and had narrowed the choice down to two promising stars. They eventually passed over Amber for a young Trisha Yearwood. But Amber was buoyed by the close call.

She was friends with Monty Powell, a powerful Nashville mover and shaker. He was producing the group *Diamond Rio* at the time and had written tons of big hits for other singers. She was already working closely with Randy Owen, the lead singer of *Alabama*. Together, Randy and Monty decided they wanted to mentor the next big country music star. Together, they knew that Amber was that person.

They headed to the studio where they recorded a demo album, a few songs that would show off Amber's talent and star power. The Maypop publishing group had heard the demo and loved it. They were behind it 100%. The plan was to take the demo to MCA and present Amber as the next big star.

The dream was almost palpable. Everything was in place. The passion Amber had pursued was within her grasp and the fulfillment was simply across town in the offices of the MCA talent executives. It was just waiting for her.

Then Amber discovered some wonderful news on a different front. She was pregnant. She and her husband had been hoping for this for years. And even better, it was twins: a boy and a girl. It seemed all the dreams were happening simultaneously. Her backers and producers decided it would be best to wait until after the children were born before they set her on the road to success.

A few months later, Taylor Ann and Chancellor were born and the first part of the dream was set. But just two weeks into the life of little Taylor Ann, she contracted spinal meningitis and severe seizures left her brain damaged and clinging to life. "Babies who are this sick, " Amber remembers the doctors telling her, "just don't live. It's just too hard."

Amber wasn't about to take that for an answer. "Here was this beautiful little baby girl I had tried for years to bring into this world, and now she was trying to leave me." So Amber had her "heart to heart" with God in a hospital bathroom. For years, she had been funneling everything she had into being a singer. "But right then, I had 'the moment.' As much as I wanted to be a singer, I wanted to be a fabulous mother even more." On a cold tile bathroom floor, she received her confirmation that she would have the chance to be exactly that. In that moment, her lifelong passion to be a singer was instantaneously replaced by her new passion to be the most "fabulous mother."

Cardiac arrest followed for little Taylor Ann. Doctors told Amber it looked grim. Brain surgery was required. Doctors told Amber to brace for the worst. "Babies who are this sick," they repeated time and time again, "just don't live." Amber was undeterred and knew better. "I would smile at them and say, 'Okay, but that's not what I'm getting.' Part of my true passion came from knowing she was still here and was still mine." She knew she had a new passion and she knew she was going to be the "most fabulous" mother.

As soon as little Taylor Ann was well enough, the family piled into the car and traveled west. She left her demo record. She left her music writing job. She left all her contacts and support system that were to help her land a contract at a big record label. That was the old support system for the old passion. "I knew I couldn't serve the music industry and this child with special needs. I had to choose."

Almost two thousand miles later, the family was surrounded by a new group. Amber's 12 brothers and sisters and extensive family would be her new support system. And here Amber focused on her new passion.

The young little family had plenty of rough times ahead. Financial and emotional struggles took their toll and eventually

Amber and her husband divorced. A bankruptcy had left them with nothing, and she, and her now three children, moved in with Amber's mother. She was swallowed up by feelings of inadequacy and overwhelmed by the thought of the future. "People came to me and asked what I was going to do, how I was going to survive. I didn't know. I didn't have a home. I didn't have a job. I didn't even have a car."

While in Nashville, Amber's mentors had been big music industry moguls. Now her mentor was entirely opposite. Her mother had been raised in Germany during World War II. She was the kind of woman who was stronger than you might imagine. She had one leg three inches shorter than the other. But she lived the mantra that "you get what you get and you don't throw a fit." She had plenty in life she could have complained about. But she didn't. "I grew up knowing that you don't look back and you don't complain. That's what my mom taught me and that's what I needed then."

As soon as Amber and her children moved in, Amber's mom put her to work. She pointed out that a cedar fence needed to be built in the backyard and Amber could begin working on that project. While Amber had certainly been handy in her life, she had never built a fence. But out she went to the backyard. "I realized I could do this. I didn't have tremendous upper body strength to dig the post holes, so I thought about it and developed a water cutter that could dig a post hole in 10 minutes. In no time at all, the fence was up and looked great."

Amber was proud of her fence, but her little German mother wasn't about to let her rest on her cedar post laurels. "You know," she pointed out. "That couch is looking a little outdated and could use some new upholstery." Hint taken. Amber ripped off the green and white 80's-looking fabric and taught herself how to tack on some basic, versatile canvas for a fresh modern look. The canvas was scarcely stapled in place when the little German voice came again. "You know, now that the couch has a new look, these chairs look like they could use a lift." Feeling bolstered by her new-found talents, Amber ripped into the

Danish modern chairs and quickly re-upholstered them in a fresh floral print.

Quickly realizing that she might spend the rest of her life fixing everything on her mother's to-do list, Amber decided to branch out. She started doing odd jobs for others. "Others," as in people who would pay her.

"I earned 200 dollars in two weeks!" she still squeals over the thought. "I was so excited. I had this additional passion to work with my hands. Years earlier, I had left this massively creative industry in Nashville, and I still yearned to do something creative. Now I was discovering how I could do that."

She started asking for power tools as gifts. At first she started just working on small projects at home. But then she branched out a little more. She can still remember her first power tool. It was a Mikita cordless screwdriver. "It was almost 20 years ago," she laughs now. "Mikita is no longer the most popular brand, but I thought it was 'the heat' at the time. I loved it."

She figured if she was going to do this, she better really do it. She got her handyman license and within two weeks, she was booked three months out. The venture took off. She branded herself as the "Fix-It Chick" and within three months, she had been snatched up by TV stations showing simple handyman projects for the homegrown handyman wannabes.

Her infectious personality and energy makes her a great TV guest. Every time I would do a segment with Amber, we would always comment on how great she was and how natural she was on TV. She could show you a snagged carpet and then whip out a crochet hook. Her fingers darted back and forth while she tucked and trimmed. She grabbed her secret tool, Super Glue and before you knew it, the snag was gone. Maybe you had a hinge or bracket at home where the screw that was holding it was coming loose from the wood. Never fear with Amber near. She had her handful of toothpicks which she could wedge into the hole. Pound 'em down. Break 'em off. Pop the screw back in and it was as tight as ever.

There was just something about her effervescent presence that made you smile. There was something about her warm demeanor that made you believe you could tackle the job yourself. There was something about her passion that simply made you want to smile and reach for a toolbox.

Amber is the perfect example of discovering new passions. Our lives change. Our circumstances change. Our priorities change. And with them, our passions change. For years, Amber's passion had been to be a singer. But in one quick whirlwind of a life experience, everything changed, including her passion.

"All of the things that have brought me so much satisfaction were from that moment when I changed my passion," she proudly states. "It all comes down to doing the things you love. These are the things that you know and give you comfort."

At first glance, it seems that Amber traded her singing passion for two different passions: mothering and handymanning. "But in reality," she is quick to point out, "they are the same. I'm doing positive things with my hands. My passion is working with my hands. I love using my hands, putting them on something that is broken and fixing it. I use my hands to make things whole and well. That's my real passion."

DARIN-ISM NO. 3

It's perfectly healthy to grow out of a passion. But what can be unhealthy is to not grow into anything else.

As I lay in my dentist's chair, Jenna, the assistant, sat nearby waiting for Dr. Marberger to show up. Dental assistants normally pull out their favorite standby questions to pass the time. So before she could ask me how many kids I had, I pulled out *my* favorite question. "What's your passion?" I asked. "You know, your favorite thing. The thing that makes you excited thinking about. The thing you would want to do if you could do anything in the world."

"It used to be dancing. I used to dance all the time. I took lots of classes and was on dance teams in school. Dancing was my passion. But it's not anymore." That's when she got a wistful look in her eyes. "I went to a dance class recently, and it just wasn't the same. So it used to be dancing, but I don't know what it is now."

Young people have a tendency to grow out of passions quickly. My oldest son, Parker, runs through about a half dozen a year. In the fall, it was break-dancing. He and a friend were so taken with it that they hired a private teacher and drove a half hour for a weekly lesson to perfect their Apple Jacks and Windmills. They spent time every day practicing, looking at break-dancing clothing, and dreaming of names for their duo. Classic passion.

That lasted about two months until injury struck. Then it was beach volleyball. He scouted out parks where they had courts that were lit at night. He would drag friends out late at night for games. Life revolved around volleyball. Another case of passion.

There was rap music up next. He downloaded a program to create rap music. He went around the house freestyling and even found a website where he offered to write rap songs for other people. I know you're stunned that no one hired him.

Then longboarding was the "newest and greatest." He designed his own longboard and cruised up and down the street, relishing in the longboarding culture. He had the clothing. He had the equipment. He had the lingo. He had the passion.

At least it's always easy to find a birthday or Christmas present for him. You just find out what the *passion du jour* is. But be prepared to see said present stashed to the side three months later, as the new passion takes over.

Maybe that's why young people are full of life. They're full of passions and always on the search for something to fill that void. They're looking for something to make them feel alive and energized. They hop from one to another, feeling the excitement and energy of trying something new. They immerse themselves in their new passion and benefit from it. It's perfectly healthy to grow out of passions. But what can be unhealthy is to NOT grow into anything else. You can abandon "a" passion, but don't abandon "all" passions. Be sure to substitute a new passion for ones that are laid down. Passions change. They don't vanish.

4

The Balsamic Bomb

You don't have to be good at Passions

2004 – the year of Fantasia. She was the bigger-than-life personality who was up against Diana DeGarmo in the American Idol Finale showdown that year. It was also the year of crazy-dancing Jon Peter Lewis, the talented, but prematurely eliminated Jennifer Hudson and the skinny, red-headed crooner, John Stevens (who reportedly was the subject of a death threat because someone REALLY wanted him eliminated). One of our family's guilty pleasures is watching American Idol. For us, that year's season was appointment TV. We didn't miss an episode. So you can imagine my excitement when I found out my boss was sending me to cover the season finale. "Guess what?" he said one day. "You're going to Hollywood," aping the show's catchphrase. I didn't squeal or fall to my knees like some of the contestants, but inside, I wanted to.

My photographer, Eric, positioned the Hollywood sign right behind me and we beamed our live shots back to the TV station. We got inside the Kodak Theatre for a rare chance to shoot video of me walking from the judges' table up to the stage. And we even got a one-on-one interview with the big guy himself: Simon Cowell.

I'll get something off my chest. I actually like Simon Cowell. Sure, he's mean spirited. Sure, he's cocky and arrogant. Sure, he wears those weird white T-shirts, which aren't flattering at all. But in spite of that, I like his acerbic, caustic critiques. Say what you like about American Idol, but you have to agree, some parts of it are pretty entertaining. Although my family might not watch the whole season, it's our tradition to watch the auditions. Admit it. It's great stuff to watch.

There was the guy named "Red" who did the worst rendition of *Bohemian Rhapsody* ever conceived. The whole thing was in falsetto and out of tune. He swore that he had gotten straight A's in high school concert choir and was sure that with Simon's coaching, he could win.

There was William Hung, whose infamous cover of Ricky Martin's *She Bangs* propelled him to a realm of mockery most of us can't imagine. He laughed before the auditions, so amazed that someone had recognized his love of singing since he was majoring in Civil Engineering, which wasn't anything like music.

There was James Lewis who loved singing. By day, he was a tour guide in Philadelphia, but when he wasn't wearing his revolutionary war costume, he was all about the music. His friends had talked him into trying out. So he showed up with his best version of, um… well… I honestly can't tell you what it was. It was purely unrecognizable. His voice sounded like a moose wailing while being put under anesthesia. Shoot video of that and then play the video in slow motion. That's what James sounded like.

The judges burst out in laughter. Even the nasty Simon briefly lost his scowl and couldn't help but laugh.

"Dog," as Randy was apt to say. "Singing just isn't your thing. We wouldn't steer you wrong. We apologize for laughing, but singing just isn't your thing."

And with that, James turned dejectedly and walked out. Outside, James was decidedly buoyant. "I'm coming back," he vowed. "Next time, I'll do something more upbeat and contemporary," he pledged as if the song choice could somehow remedy the voice.

Constantly throughout the auditions, we heard dejected hopefuls plead with the judges, "This is my passion." They beg, "You can't do this to me. This is what I love. I live to sing. This is what I was meant to do. Please, you gotta' believe me. This is my life!"

I believe them. It sounds like classic passion. You can feel the passion in their emotions. You can see the passion in their expressions and tears. You can hear the passion in their voices. Unfortunately, you can't hear any talent in their voices to go along with it.

It doesn't matter. Ability does NOT go hand in hand with passion. You DON'T have to be great at something to have a passion. You don't have to be "the best" to be passionate. Passion does not mean perfection.

The benefits from having and exercising our passions are actually kind of selfish. We're the ones with the passions. We're the ones who benefit largely from exploring them.

"It's impossible," said Pride.
"It's risky," said Experience.
"It's pointless," said Reason.

"Give it a try," whispered the Heart.

I had been working at a TV station in Lewiston, Idaho when I returned home to the San Francisco Bay Area for a family summer vacation. While there, I spotted something on TV about some audition for the host of *Wheel of Fortune*. "What's that about?" I asked my sister who still lived at home.

"Haven't you heard?" she seemed stunned. This clearly was the biggest news of the century and I had somehow missed out on it. "Pat Sajak is leaving his daytime version of the *Wheel of Fortune* to do a new nighttime talk show. So they're holding auditions to find the new host of the daytime game show."

Then her eyes popped open even more and her eyelids shot up. "You have to audition!" she screamed. "It's perfect. You're here in town and the auditions are in two days over in San Francisco. Hey everyone, Darin is going to audition for *Wheel of Fortune!* He's going to be famous."

Sure, she was jumping the gun just a bit. She already had me hosting the show, and I hadn't even decided if I was going to audition. After thinking it over, I figured it would be fun. At least it would be something to tell people when they asked what I did for my summer vacation. And nothing concrete was planned for that day of my vacation anyway.

So on the day in question, I drove over the Bay Bridge to San Francisco and tracked down the Hyatt Hotel where the search began for the new replacement. I parked and walked into the lobby where I spotted someone near a *Wheel of Fortune* sign. I asked him where the auditions were taking place. "Up on the third floor," he answered for what clearly must have been the bajillionth time. I turned toward the elevator to head up a couple flights, when the attendant broke back in. "Um, sir, the line starts down here." And with that, he pointed down a long hall lined with dozens of hopefuls.

As it turned out, the line started there, snaked up the stairs, wound around the second floor, before finally heading up to the third floor. Once there, you still had to wait through another labyrinth of halls filled with more Sajak-wannabes. I had plenty of time all afternoon to size up my competition. I watched their mannerisms. I noticed their clothing. I analyzed their quiet self-conversations. I tried to figure out what had brought them there, and what skills they brought along with them.

When the actual audition arrived, they ushered us in groups of ten into a large convention hall where there was a panel of TV types sitting behind a banquet table.

Someone at the table introduced who they were and then asked us to do the same. "We'd like you to briefly tell us who you are and something interesting about you. We'll start at this end of the line and just take 30 seconds to let us get to know you."

I certainly don't remember everyone in the group, but I can still recall two in particular.

The first one stated his name and explained that he was a bread delivery truck driver. He was in his 40's, short and overweight. His clothes looked like they were the ones he might have worn to work that morning. "I really like *Wheel of Fortune*," he stammered. "And I think I would be good on the show." He paused, then added sheepishly, with eyes darting between the floor and back of the room, "and I would like to meet Vanna." With that, he stepped back into his place in the line.

Here was a guy who was clearly out of his league. He wasn't going to have anyone looking over their shoulder, worried about the competition. He was a nighttime bread deliveryman. Now, I'm sure he was great at his job. If I ever need a hoagie bun or a loaf of split-buttertop, I'm calling this guy without a second of hesitation. But he had waited hours in line because he thought he could be good at this. He clearly had some motivating (although severely misguided) passion and that's what got him to stand up in front of some TV executives and tell them he should be the next Pat Sajak.

Then there was another guy who must have been in his late 20's. He took a step forward, stated his name and then, "I work on the weekends down at a club here in San Francisco. It's sort of a cabaret club and I'm a performer there. I do impressions of some famous female performers. And," he added slyly, "I'm pretty good at it."

I was a little shocked. What was this guy thinking? He somehow thought his experience as a cross-dressing singer qualified him to host one of the most successful game shows in history. Did he figure he could be both Pat and Vanna at the same time? Maybe save the show some money since he could do double duty? But somehow, when he looked in the mirror that morning (assuming he was looking at the male version and not the female version) he saw something that made him believe in his passion.

While I was a bit surprised at the group that been assembled in that room, I was amazed at their passion. Clearly something made them get up that day, get to San Francisco and wait for hours for their shot. They weren't any good. But it didn't matter. They were driven to be there. They got butterflies in their stomach anticipating the moment. And even though they left with nothing more than the "lovely parting gift" of a *Wheel of Fortune* pencil, they still had that drive. For all I know, now, 25 years later they still have similar dreams.

Good for them. They acted on their passion. They had an experience. And that's more than can be said for all the others who might have had the passion but feared they didn't have what it takes to back it up. Those people didn't have an experience.

DARIN-ISM NO. 4

Don't confuse a skill set with a passion.

One of the most gifted TV cooking guests I have encountered is Laura Wolford. I remember the first time she came on TV and we got to cook. It was a roller coaster ride. She had tremendous energy and enthusiasm. She was a natural on TV and exuded her passion for cooking, not to mention her passion for passion. At first I thought it was just my opinion, but then others began to notice. From the way she added ingredients, to the way she sampled the sauces, from the way she stirred, to the way she described the ingredients, there was just this electricity about her segments.

Laura's specialty was creating simple dishes that were wonderful. She taught the basic elements of cooking and showed how to apply them. She showed how simple it was to make a roux, and then, in about the time it took to lick your lips, she had transformed it into three different sauces, one of them spiked with balsamic vinegar. She could show you how simple it was to roast vegetables, and then before you could grab a carrot peeler, she would highlight the best vegetables for roasting, whip them out of the oven and drizzle some balsamic vinegar on top of them. Or she could show how to grill unusual items like fruits. She would pull out some quartered pineapples, halved plums and sliced bananas and show what can happen when they meet up with a grill, and of course a splash of balsamic vinegar.

Laura, we discovered, had a penchant for balsamic vinegar.

She also had a knack for gaining inspiration from things that would give the rest of us fear. Nothing was too great a challenge for her. So I came up with the idea of how to tap into her passion. We would stage what we called an "Ambush Dinner." We would send a camera and Laura out to some unsuspecting person who was bored with cooking dinner night after night. Laura would then have free reign to rummage around the kitchen, pantry, fridge and anywhere else food might be stashed, to see what she could find. She then had the challenge to come up with some creative dinner the family had never had before, but would end up loving. Laura loved the challenge. Viewers loved watching her mind at work.

December rolled around and I suggested that we take a holiday bent on the idea. We would send Laura out on a Cookie Ambush. We found a family in the middle of Christmas cookie making and timed it so she would invade them mid-cookie baking. Then with some things they already had (or that she might have conveniently brought along) she would take their cookies to new heights.

She mixed pecans and pretzels in with chocolate chip cookie dough and baked it in a loaf pan. She tucked sweetened peanut butter centers inside a ball of sugar cookie dough. She stirred fruitcake fruits, macadamia nuts, and coconut into basic cookie dough to make a tropical treat. She whipped up a whole plate full of mouth watering Christmas cookies.

We had taped the whole process and were getting ready to air it when it hit us. There was nothing with balsamic vinegar. Balsamic vinegar had sort of become Laura's trademark. She found an excuse to use it in pretty much everything she had created on the show. And now, here we were on the verge of a Laura Wolford segment, and there was not a drop of balsamic vinegar to be found.

That's when we realized the ultimate challenge. Could Laura make a cookie with balsamic vinegar? We had never thrown a challenge at her that she hadn't risen to tackle. We issued the idea. Laura grabbed it up.

The idea was to air the pre-taped piece with Laura at the cookie baking home. Then we would be in the studio live to show how to make Laura's most unusual and original creation, The Balsamic Bomb (the name was Laura's idea).

The cooking segment was thoroughly entertaining. We watched Laura rifling through cupboards, melting chocolate and smashing hard candies. Then Laura unveiled her newest creation, a cookie with balsamic vinegar. She started with a basic shortbread cookie dough, then stirred in some dried cranberries, chopped pistachios, and finally, that magical elixir Laura thinks of as the juice of life, balsamic vinegar.

We tasted them.

On paper it was great. In our mouths, not so much.

It wasn't like I had to run to the garbage can and spit it out. But it wasn't like my eyes rolled around in the back of my head in delirium either. The cookie was interesting, but more "bomb" than "balsamic." While other Laura recipes had people running to the website to download them by the thousands, the Balsamic Bomb was barely a blip.

It didn't matter to Laura. Her passion for food hadn't diminished. In spite of the lack of victory for vinegar, she still forged on. She continued to try foods in new and unusual ways. She didn't care if the cookie wasn't the greatest; she went on trying to find something that was. And had she not, we might not have discovered one her most flavorful creations, using powdered Jell-o as a dry rub for grilled chicken.

Her passion was the same whether her recipes were smash hits or nose dive failures. Her success didn't determine her passion. And her failures didn't either.

One thing life has taught me: If you are interested, you never have to look for new interests. They come to you.
When you are genuinely interested in one thing, it will always lead to something else.
-Eleanor Roosevelt

Of all the people I have interviewed or conducted segments with on TV, Becky Low is likely the most prolific. She is the epitome of a kind and mentoring Home Ec teacher. She knows all the tricks of the trade when it comes to the kitchen. And for years, Becky was a Friday staple. One year, we checked to see which online segments had been viewed the most on our website. Of the hundreds and hundreds of segments, Becky had two that landed in the top 10. Whether it was the secret to soft Christmas sugar cookies, or how to make fluffy rolls at Thanksgiving, Becky always had the secrets.

Becky had a passion for food, and it showed. She had discovered it early on, as a child. She loves working with food and teaching about food. But not all of Becky's run-ins with her passion have been successful.

Becky wasn't always whipping out knock-off Olive Garden recipes or Bridal Shower Ribbon Sandwiches on TV segments. Instead, one of the most memorable lessons she learned in pursuing her passion came while she was a Home Ec. major in college. She was the secretary for the campus Physical Plant. This was where all the electrical and plumbing and maintenance workings were taken care of. Becky was a secretary while working her way through school at Utah State University.

USU is situated in the picturesque Cache Valley settled by resourceful pioneers more than a century earlier. Many of those early settlers had to plant what they could. They had discovered that the Potawatomi Plum was easy to transport across the plains and grew fairly easily. So, the Cache Valley was dotted with stands of winter-hardy Potawatomi plums. These aren't the typical plums you're used to finding in your local grocery store. They're not as large. They're not as purple. They're not as good.

One day, a plumber walked into the physical plant with the exciting news that he knew of a large stand of plum trees that were just loaded with plums. They were literally "ripe for the pickin." Becky was intrigued. This was a rare opportunity. "There are about 15 Potawatomi plum trees out in a field," he announced as Becky's eyes got bigger. "Anyone who wants 'em can just go pick 'em."

The thought of free plums was just too much to resist. She thought of her resourceful mother and wondered what she would do in a case like this. She was sure that the right thing to do was to go start picking Potawatomi plums. So she and a friend headed out to the large field with the dense stand of plum trees. "Now I'm not a big fan of plums," she confessed. "But I'm a big fan of free."

So Becky and her friend picked. They picked and picked and picked. They filled up bags. They packed up boxes. They picked until they could pick no more. And then they headed for home. But what had started out as a great idea now turned into a quandary. What in the world was she going to do with all those plums? Even after picking pecks of the plums, she still didn't like them. She was in a Potawatomi plum predicament. She finally settled on making jam.

Now as much as she didn't like plums, she didn't like jam even more. But what else is there to do with piles of Potawatomies? So she set to work making perhaps the biggest batch of Potawatomi jam the county had ever seen. While the plums had been free, the rest of the supplies certainly were not.

Few students have a huge supply of canning jars on hand, and Becky was no exception. She headed to the store and bought up huge amounts of jars and lids and rims. She purchased bags and bags of sugar along with all the pectin to make the jam. And then, with her savings invested in canning supplies, she headed home.

She transformed her home into a mini-Smucker's factory. She peeled and pitted and pitted and peeled. She mixed and stirred and cooked in giant pots over hot stoves. "It was a mess," she laughs. "I made jam. I made more jam. I made even more jam. And I just had a little, tiny college apartment. I didn't have much room. And the jam just took over." Soon, the jam was all neatly packed into the shiny new jars. The shiny new jars were packed away in boxes. And the boxes were packed away, well, they were packed away anywhere Becky could find room for them in her tiny apartment. In this case, it was dozens of jars of jam stashed in a coat closet. Coats could be hung elsewhere. The preserves took precedent.

This "jamapalooza" had all transpired during the spring of Becky's senior year. And now, as the year drew to a close, Becky was graduating and heading off to her first teaching job a few hundred miles away in Idaho. It was back in the days when you could move with all your stuff in your car and Becky hadn't acquired too much stuff, so she started packing up her life.

She had a used Pontiac Catalina. It was a beautiful green color with the front part of the hood that jutted out to cut the air as it sped along. It was a big boat of a car, big enough to hold a college student's life possessions. Becky packed up her apartment until she came to her stash of Potawatomi jam. She had made jars and jars of it, and hadn't eaten a bite, and had to decide what to do with it all. Since there was a little bit of extra room in her big boat of a Catalina, she packed it in. She filled every available spot in the car with her prized Potawatomi, and now, with her car laden down with jam, she sped off to Carey, Idaho where the plums took up residence in a vacant back bedroom.

The job in Carey soon led to a job in southern Nevada. So she packed up all her possessions in the Catalina, including all those jars of Potawatomi plum jam, and headed south. Her first residence was a minuscule house with no storage. But she found a spot in the corner of the screened-in back porch where the Potawatomi was tucked away. She then moved to a trailer where the jars sat on the floor of a broom closet smack dab in the middle of the Nevada desert for two more years.

Becky took an assignment that took her out of the state for a couple years. She couldn't take the Potawatomi with her, so they had to find a new home. Her parents offered to babysit the Potawatomies while she was gone, so back they went to Beaver. The cases were stashed in the basement.

When she returned to teaching, she headed out to Panguitch for another job, and the jam jars tagged along, too. Becky was getting tired of tucking the boxes out of site. So they just were sprawled across the floor in an extra bedroom for the Panguitch stay.

Then, after another couple years, she moved again, back to Beaver. She had an old house, with an old wash house in back. It was damp and musty and the perfect spot for some jars of jam.

Finally, after a decade of traipsing from city to city, and dragging the cases of jam with her, she took stock of her prized Potawatomi Plum jam. It was all still there. "Oh, maybe I had opened one jar over the course of the 10 years. It wasn't like I actually even ate that jar. I might open it and it would just sit in the fridge until I would finally have to throw it out. I just don't like jam. And I certainly don't like plum jam."

And with that revelation, she got out all of the boxes she had been dragging around for 10 years. One by one, she opened the jars, and scraped out the contents into a big garbage can. And without a twinge of regret, she drove to the dump and gave the jam a final resting place.

Driving back home from the dump, she thought about the jam. It hadn't been a waste to pick peck after peck of plums. It hadn't been a waste to practice the resourcefulness of making jam from surplus fruit. And it hadn't been a waste to learn how to can jar after jar of it. (Now dragging it around from city to city might have been a little bit of a waste.) Food and Home Economics were her passion. She had fed those passions even though she had never eaten so much as a jar of the jam. And with the glow of Potawatomi Plum jam in the rearview mirror, she was glad for the experience.

If you're going to be passionate about something, be passionate about learning. And if you're going to hate something, hate the false idea that you are not capable of your dreams.
~ Daniel Golston

I have been golfing once in my adult life. (That doesn't include the golfing outings with the windmills and the loop-the-loop holes.) Ron Nimmer was the sports anchor at the TV station where I was working and he was a golfing fan. At the time, I was the station's weathercaster. Since we both worked evening shifts, he suggested that we play a round of golf one morning. I eventually ran out of excuses and figured I would accompany him for a round.

We met at the appointed tee time, I rented my set of golf clubs, and under his tutelage, we headed out to the course. I was horrendous. I don't know what I shot. But it was well into the three digits. I didn't know how to use my drivers. I didn't know how to use my wedges. I didn't know how to use my irons. I knew how to use the putters, thanks to my experience on the miniature golf courses and those treacherous castles with the raising and lowering drawbridges. But my putting game wasn't enough to save me. Although it was 20 years ago, I can still remember my best hit of the day. It was my second swing on a relatively easy par 3. I was only about 20 yards from the tee since my tee shot hadn't gone quite as far as I had pictured. But my second swing actually connected. It took off and sailed about a hundred yards. It landed pretty much in the middle of the fairway. What, even for other duffers would have been a less than stellar drive, was the most beautiful shot of the morning. It was what I pictured most of my drives doing, even though it was the only one of the day that actually did.

For a moment, I glimpsed what golfing could be. It was that one drive that often hooks many aspiring golfers. But I didn't bite. It didn't interest me at all.

Flash forward 20 years. I now have a teen-aged son who has discovered golf. We used to live near a par-3 golf course. If you're not into golfing, this is a mini-version of a real golf course. There are no long fairways. It's mostly a tee-shot, a chip shot to get it on the green, and then an easy putt for the hole-in. My son was younger when he decided he wanted to be the next Tiger Woods. There were some basic hereditary obstacles, but we headed to the nearby course to let him give it a try. It was the English Springs course, just outside Louisville, Kentucky. There were clean-cut greens surrounded by white gable fences tucked into the gently rolling hills. And there, on a late spring afternoon my son, Norm, had his first experience with what he was sure was going to be his new love.

He shanked and sliced to his heart's content. I was his personal caddy. The idea is that I would just tag along with his bag of clubs and keep him company. I ended up spending most of the time digging through bushes trying to figure out where his errant drive had landed. I spent a fair amount of time raking out the bunkers after other shots ended up in the "sand box." And I stood around scouring the rough to find where his ball had ended up. There was one particularly harrowing hole. Hole #5 had a small pond with an evil spirit. All you had to do was pop the ball up and over the water to land 70 yards away on the green. Sounds simple enough. But the small pond with the white flagstone outcroppings lining the far end, had it in for unsuspecting novices. It liked to swallow up errant balls the way you and I gobble up popcorn. Norm got out his favorite ball and proceeded to hit it directly into the water. He tried again. Same resting place. A third swing had the exact same result.

I wasn't too surprised. The golfing nut doesn't fall far from the tree, and I assumed he had inherited his old man's propensity for golf. I had tried golfing and discovered I was horrendous. I had given it a fair shot, but it did nothing for me. My guess was that I was witnessing the same thing happening with my son. But it was nothing like that. It didn't matter how many balls ended up in the water or mud or rough or sand or thickets. He was hooked. Somehow, it didn't matter to him that he hadn't hit the fairway on most of his shots. He didn't mind. He had smelled the freshly mown grass of a golf course. He had felt the solid contact of a club hitting the multi-dimpled golf ball. And he had heard the plunk of that little white ball when it drops in the cup.

That's all it took for him. Somewhere out on the 9 holes, his heart had become engaged with his actions. It didn't matter that he wasn't any good. He didn't pay attention to that.

We had both gone golfing. We both had the same type of score that embarrasses most people. But the results were opposite. I walked away, never to even longingly wish to be out on the course. He was only temporarily satiated and could hardly wait to get back at it. He watched golf on TV. He subscribed to magazines. He searched online for the latest golf clubs. He researched which balls went the farthest. And he looked forward to his next encounter with his greatest nemesis, the pond on Hole #5.

Norm had found his passion even though he was no good at what he was doing. Skill level has nothing to do with whether we love something or not. We had both tried golfing. For me, in spite of my one stellar drive, my heart had never connected and golf wasn't something I was interested in. For my son, who lost half a box of balls to the high seas on Hole #5, it was the most exhilarating experience ever. His heart was harnessed up and ready to run.

For the record, he got to the point where he faced down the pond and ended up winning most of the time. He even went on to become the captain of his high school golf team. I just say that so he doesn't get humiliated by his friends, picturing him getting beaten by a water hazard. But it wouldn't really matter. He could still be out there slugging away, watching balls taking a dive every time he tees up. He discovered a passion for golf, regardless of his ability. He wasn't denied his love for his game simply because he wasn't any good. Certainly, most of us know a would-be golfer who is really more of a weekend hacker. They can still love something even though they might not be any good. Our passions aren't dictated by how well we master the activity. They are dictated by how much our heart is engaged.

I glanced at someone's blog one day and spotted what I thought was a misguided assumption. The author was talking about passions and how people should use them. She wrote that we need to be doing what we are good at, and what we have gifts for. "Those," she stated, "are our passions."

When I related it to my son, he scrunched up his eyes. "Those aren't passions ," he scowled. "That's a skill set."

Don't confuse your skill sets with your passions. Skills are great and you can benefit the world and those around you with them. But your passions are more important. They benefit something more important: your own well-being and your happiness.

You don't have to be Steve Jobs. You don't have to be Mother Teresa. You don't have to be Willy Wonka. Don't worry about how successful you are or how much of an influence you will have on others. You just have to be you.

Your passions, no matter how good you are at them, benefit you.

5

Teaching Art In Acid-Washed Denim

Others can benefit from your Passions

The shrill ring of the phone jolted my eyes open early one September morning.

It wasn't particularly early for most of the rest of the world. A 6:45 AM wake up call would be considered "sleeping in" for many parents needing to get their kids up and out the door to school. It certainly wouldn't be unexpected for anyone heading out to the corporate world to slog through another day pushing papers and punching time cards. But I didn't belong to those groups. I was newly-married, childless, and enjoying my late shift at the TV station where I didn't head into work until 3 PM. So why in the world would someone be calling me at the unheard of hour of "anything before noon?"

"Mr. Adams?" came the calm woman's voice over the receiver. "We have a 3rd grade class at Bonneville Elementary School for you today. School starts at 8:00. Would that work out for you?"

I was instantly awake.

This was the morning I had been waiting for. I was now officially a substitute school teacher.

I jumped out of bed and started getting ready. My wife, who was still finishing up her last year of classes at the university, was trying to figure out why I was rushing to beat her out the door. I could feel a twinge of excitement as I tried to determine my most pressing questions. Was my acid-washed denim jacket appropriate attire for a substitute teacher? Should I play my new Erasure CD during lunch to look hip? What were the names of the four Teenage Mutant Ninja Turtles?

One of my passions is teaching. I had known that for a while. So, since my regular job of predicting weather for most of southeast Idaho at 5 PM and 10PM didn't need me most days until later on, I had decided that I could indulge my teaching passion and be a substitute school teacher from time to time. And this particular morning was the first of those times.

Bonneville Elementary School was just a few blocks away, but I made a detour to the grocery store to stock up on a few bulk bags of Tootsie Rolls and Smarties. I wasn't about to go into that unknown den of 3rd graders unprepared. I stocked up on all the bribes I could need.

Armed with my treats, I greeted the day and 27 3rd graders, who normally call Mrs. Dixon their teacher, as they stormed in the door mere seconds after 8:00 AM. Although I was certainly a little apprehensive to start, I settled in a groove. Math went fine. As long as I was tossing out candy for right answers, it was shocking how enthusiastic the class participation was. I made it through Reading. Those kids kept their noses buried in their books as long as I kept dropping random sweets on their desks. And as they dashed off to lunch, I regrouped for the second half of the day.

The morning had been mostly required subjects, but the afternoon had a more exciting elective: art. I'm certainly no Renoir or Rembrandt. But the idea of teaching an art project was somehow exhilarating and exciting. It wasn't like I was going to be teaching subtraction and borrowing, or whatever they call it nowadays. This wasn't a class in reflexive pronouns which still trip up most adults. No. This was art. You can't go wrong with art. This was just about inspiring influential minds. That's the exact part of teaching that connects with my passion.

The lesson Mrs. Dixon had written up was technically on Monet. I was to teach about the history of the impressionist era and other artists who were contemporaries of Monet. The assignment was to have each child create a piece of art using small, torn scraps of colored construction paper. At first blush, it looked pretty cut and dry, or in this case, rip and dry.

But that was only how the average, non-passionate mind would look at it. For me, it was the highlight of the day. When the day resumed, I showed some of the greatest Monet paintings and some other famous pieces to illustrate what impressionist art looked like. From a distance, the pieces looked like a castle, or a cliff, or a pond. But then, I made the kids get up close and see how the paintings were made up of nothing more than blobs and spots of intense colors. They got excited the more we broke down the paintings into their abstract makeup.

Then the really fun part started. The kids ripped up sheet after sheet after sheet of colored paper. And then the pasting began.

I remember child after child coming up to me showing me their creation which invariably consisted of about 20% of their white paper covered with colored scraps.

"Get back and cover it with more color!" I would bellow in a good-natured way.

They would give it another try and return with their more heavily embellished paper.

"I can still see white! Do you see any white on Monet's painting?" I would once again chide them with a chuckle. "Cover it all up!"

Little by little, they caught the impressionist inspiration. White slowly started disappearing. Colored scraps started piling up thicker. By the end of the assignment, beaming faces were anxious to get my smile of approval as they held up their papers which were about 5 times heavier than they had been when they started. The colored scraps got thicker and thicker as the mini-masterpieces took on a Monet-esque flair. The kids had caught on to the assignment I had been trying to drill into their little noggins.

I can still remember the afternoon of art. It was something I had been passionate about and I loved teaching the topic and encouraging the kids to create in a non-conforming way. For the next couple of days, I still thought about how much I had enjoyed teaching the art project. It was much more fun than I had expected my day of substitute teaching to be. It had been a passion high for me and I knew that I had been the one to benefit.

A few days later, I was called to substitute for another class at Bonneville. As I was leaving at the end of the day, I thought I would pop my head in to say "hi" to Mrs. Dixon, the teacher of the class I had first substituted for.

Her eyes lit up. I thought she would give me a hard time for bribing the kids with Tootsie Rolls. I worried she might chide me for not marking the attendance roll properly. I figured she had discovered something I hadn't done like all the other substitute teachers.

"I have to tell you something," she started. "What you taught those kids about Monet and art was something else." I was a little worried about what that "something else" was. "It was amazing," she continued. "They are still talking about it. They couldn't wait to show me when I got back. They have been so proud of their creations ever since they made them."

And then she leaned in a little. "They will never forget what you taught them here that day."

How could that be? I was just exercising my passion. I was just doing what I loved. I was just engaging what I loved. I figured I was the beneficiary.

But that's one of the residual things that happens with passions. Others get caught up in the wake and ride along with you and your passions. Other people can benefit from them. We start out thinking that we are the ones who have the passions and we are the ones who gain the most. But while our passions benefit us, they can benefit others, too.

And generally, the more passionate we are, the more other

people can get caught up in that influential passion pulse.

Do what you love.
You'll be better at it.

- *Francis Ford Coppola*

Colder weather was settling in each night bringing with it the anticipation of the upcoming holidays. It was October and the fall colors were at their peak. From her office, Home Economist Teresa Hunsaker could see the vibrant display on the mountains to the east. It's the time of year that most of us look forward to with at least a twinge of anticipation and excitement.

Not so for the family of four who walked in on that particular October.

They entered quietly and sat down across the desk from Teresa. A paralyzing fear had overcome them and they weren't sure where to turn.

It had been a couple days earlier that Teresa had received a call from a Riverdale City administrator. The Larsons (name changed) needed help. The city had been beckoning young families from all around and the affordable housing prices and family-friendly atmosphere were an easy call to heed. The Larsons, with their two young children settled right in.

They had purchased their first home. It was a smaller, yet modern and stylish home tucked back into the quiet end of a subdivision with plenty of other similar families. It was perfect for 3-year old Sophie and 9-month old Tyler. Scott was a successful engineer at a local company that manufactured airbags for cars. Lisa worked part-time at the local Target store. Between the two of them, they pulled down close to 80-thousand dollars a year, certainly ample for the small family of four.

Life was idyllic for a few years. Just when the Larsons thought everything was going their way, the economy hit a rough patch. When the airbag company downsized, Scott found himself unemployed. But he was a competent and hard worker and they were sure he would land another good-paying job in no time. There was no reason to panic just yet.

Through the spring, he searched for another good-paying engineering job. Unfortunately, he found himself competing against a growing number of other unemployed engineers, anxious for the few openings that popped up. In between job searching, he worked the neighborhood picking up whatever odd jobs he could. Tiffany increased her hours at Target, trying to help bring in whatever she could to pay the bills.

They had gone from a comfortable 80-thousand dollars a year to a stifling 15-thousand dollars and the bills were piling up. They paid what they could, and the others got pushed to the back. They kept thinking something would happen, but the only thing happening was they were falling deeper in debt with no plan for the future. Instead of trying to immediately get help, they silently hunkered down and hoped.

By the time a friend who was a city administrator discovered the situation, it was clearly serious. The Larsons had been delivered a foreclosure notice and many bills were to the point of going to collection. The city wanted to preserve the atmosphere of the community and quality of life and they had become proactive about helping families in financial trouble by directing them to the proper resources.

That's why Teresa's phone had rung on that October afternoon. And that's why the Larsons were now sitting across the desk from her. "They weren't in shock, but pretty close. They were just immobile and didn't know what to do," Teresa remembers of that October afternoon.

For me and thousands of TV viewers, we recognized Teresa as the Home Economist who knew that meat tenderizer could get perspiration stains out of shirts. She knew the best place to get batteries and pregnancy tests was at the dollar store. And the self-proclaimed "queen of bleach" knew everything you could do with bleach including killing weeds, keeping cut flowers alive and disinfecting cell phones. She was the consummate homemaking expert who had all the answers.

But there was another side of Teresa that few people knew. It was the side of her that saved people from financial disaster. And this foreclosure intervention and debt mitigation was where Teresa could make a significant impact. It was her passion to help people who were in the most dire of situations. As gutwrenching as it could be, it was where there was the greatest potential to see the results of her passion.

"I love it," Teresa gushed. "I love it. Sure there are other things that I do. There's the canning or the cleaning or other things. But teaching financial tools is just very rewarding. The finances...it's just where the rubber meets the road. It's where you can have a real and lasting impact."

She looked at the Larsons with her kind, understanding eyes and knew exactly where they were coming from. "They were so young and so afraid. They were facing the very real possibility that they could lose everything. It was frightening to watch."

But Teresa couldn't reveal her own fear for them. "I had to tell them that it's possible. They could get out debt. 'We can stop this ball from rolling. I need you to do this, and do it exactly as I tell you.' I had to get them to a place where they could think and know that it was possible, that there was someone who could walk them through it and it was going to be manageable. It was going to be okay."

Next, she asked for, and got, a detailed rundown of all their expenses. Then she poured over the receipts and statements with an eagle eye and a sharp pencil.

The main street in Riverdale is filled with easy temptations. They have big signs with familiar names like Applebee's, Chili's, and Wendy's. "Those names were popping up a little too often on their bank statements. It was one of the first things I noticed. And it was one of the first things to cut out of the budget."

Teresa then turned her attention to the grocery bills. As it so happened, Lisa had been doing a fair amount of food shopping at Target. After her shift, she would stroll over to the food aisles and pick up whatever caught her eye. It was easy to do, but she ended up buying far more food than she needed.

"I saw that they were spending well over 500 dollars a month on food. And that's for a small family of four. Little Tyler wasn't even a year old, so he wasn't eating that much. But Lisa wasn't used to cooking from a menu, so we planned it out and she committed to only buying what she needed. They cut that grocery bill down to under 200 dollars a month. That's a savings of over 300 dollars a month," Teresa was quick to point out in case someone was mathematically impaired.

They did everything Teresa asked of them. They sold some of their possessions. Lisa abandoned her manicures. Scott cut back on cigarettes. They cut their cable TV. They followed her every directive, anxious for whatever she could do to help them salvage their lives.

They had to write a "letter of hardship" to their lenders, explaining their situation and what they were doing. "It's a pretty tall order. You have to have all your t's crossed and your i's dotted. And you have to come up with a pretty hefty amount of money to show that you're working in the right direction. It's a very difficult thing to do. But as frightened as they had been, they didn't flinch. It was really a monumental task for them. And they did it!

It was a long, arduous journey that took place over most of an entire year. But little by little, Teresa helped them reverse the tide and start paying off all their debts. Scott eventually got another job, and the young family could see the light at the end of the tunnel.

Teresa had mapped out the plan to escape financial doom, and the Larsons had followed it to the letter. They had appealed to lenders. They had cut eating out. They had mapped out their groceries. She loved seeing the progress they were making and realizing her guidance had made an impact. They had slowly, but steadily clawed their way out. They had done exactly as she had told them, and it had turned out exactly as she had promised.

And then one day, as summer was pressing into fall, she got a note in the mail. It was from the Larsons.

It was a heartfelt note expressing their appreciation to Teresa for being their light in their darkest hour. They had been paralyzed with fear when Teresa had stepped in. In the note, they told her they would be forever grateful to her. For almost a full year, she had taken them by the hand and showed them exactly what steps to take. She had saved them.

Since then, Teresa has seen the Larsons several times. They have another child now and the family of five is on solid ground. And every time they see her, they are so appreciative of what she did for them.

"It's wonderful," Teresa reflects, and then echoes a little quieter, "It's just wonderful."

I fall in love with people's passion, the way their eyes light up when they talk about the thing they love and the way they fill with light.
-Melissa Cox

The melting butter was bubbling with the dark brown sugar as the smell of cinnamon wrapped around the TV studio. Our recipe of the day was Cinnamon Caramel Corn with Pecans and White Chocolate. See. I have your attention already.

That's exactly the idea. Sara Wells had whipped up the recipe that we simply called Cinnamon Bun Popcorn. It was just like one of those gooey, sticky cinnamon rolls you get in the mall, except this was in the form of a popcorn. It was brilliant.

But that's what you expect from the "Best Bites" girls. Sara and her friend Kate Jones had started up the blog "Our Best Bites" a short time before and it had exploded, filled with recipes for anything you have a hankering for. There were Chocolate Chip Cookie Dough Truffles, Gooey Cookie Pie Bites and Ice Cream Crunch Bars. Okay, so they weren't all sweets. Those are just the ones that jumped out at me. You can find other more nutritious recipes like Baked Chicken-Bacon Alfredo, Cowboy

Quesadillas, and Grilled BBQ Pulled Pork Pizza. With a lineup like that, it's bound to be a hit.

Sara and Kate were regulars in our kitchen, or at least as regular as their schedule would permit them to travel from their respective states. They shined the light on their concept for a hot chocolate bar. They showed us the technique for making a penguin cupcake topper out of marshmallows. They showed us how to make creamy chicken tacquitos. Sara and Kate were the rock stars of the cooking blog world. People around the world turned to the duo for their recipes and tutorials.

But their culinary passion had started out as something much less ambitious than that.

"Kate and I just started the blog totally as a hobby to work on. We both had little babies and we needed something extra. While we were trying to figure out what that might be, it dawned on me that Kate already had a blog. It seemed like the natural thing to do."

Kate had started a little blog earlier just to stay in touch with family. It was just a personal little blog and she had shared some recipes on it. And with that, the idea for the Best Bites girls was born.

"We both loved food. It was something we were passionate about. And we loved sharing recipes with other people and teaching them how to make things," Sara remembered. It was just a natural progression to start a blog.

"I still remember the very first post I ever did. It was about paninis," Sara proudly remembers. "It was before paninis were super popular. I was ahead of the curve. Back then, you could only get paninis in restaurants and I was really good at them."

"I had to figure out something for that first post, and I considered myself as an expert at paninis. It was my specialty." So she whipped up her first ever blog post. It was about cheese. It was about tomatoes. It was about what you could do with paninis. The obvious thing would be to stick them in your mouth, but Kate was able to come up with more options than just *eating them.*

She took some inspiration from a smoked turkey and artichoke panini she had just eaten at Paradise Bakery. Looking back on it, it really wasn't much of a post. She took some photos of artichoke hearts artfully laid on the turkey and swiss cheese. She charred the bread "just so" and posed the sandwich with some fresh basil leaves on a stark white plate. She mentioned some tips about tomatoes or cheese or some herb mayo spread and called it good.

And with that panini post, the blog was born. By that time, Sara had moved to Boise and Kate's husband was finishing up school and they were getting ready to move to Louisiana. So began Sara's catharsis.

You see, Sara actually did the blog partly for herself. She had felt overwhelmed by some of the things she would have to do forever. There were times when she felt like a bad wife or a bad mom and the "Our Best Bites' blog was a turning point for her. It started with just general cooking information, with a subtle seasoning of how it had affected her life and made her a better person.

As the recipes continued to flow from Sara and Kate, the followers grew. There were plenty of other moms, just like them, who wanted to know "What's for dinner?" It was Sara's passion for cooking and sharing her love of cooking that kept her going. She, like so many of us when we are engaged in our passions, figured she was the main one benefitting.

And then, the first letter came.

It was from a typical mom who had discovered the "Our Best Bites" blog.

"I can still remember the impact of that letter, although I can't remember all the details," Sara searches the past. "She might have been from Utah. I'm not really sure. But she was just a typical mom. And she was writing a "thank you for your blog" letter. I didn't know there was such a thing.

"This blog follower had felt overwhelmed. It wasn't like she was a bad cook, she just felt the weight of this daunting task hanging over her head every day. She was tired of trying to think of something her kids might like. And they didn't like a lot of things. Every day she had to come up with something, and most of the time, she felt it was a failure."

And then one day, this nameless mom from Everytown, USA struck the mother lode. She had someone giving her ideas, and ideas her family would eat and like. "Suddenly, her life changed. She discovered ways to involve her kids in the kitchen. Her kids could help her make food. And they would eat it! She wrote to us, thanking us for changing her life," Sara's voice picked up with excitement. "She finally felt like a great mom. She finally felt like she was a success in the kitchen. Dinner was finally fun."

Since that first "thank you for your blog" letter, there have been more, many more. That first exasperated mom wasn't the only one out there. There were plenty more who wrote in, and far more who never did. There was a veritable army of Best Biters who were learning to love cooking and mastering the techniques they had never learned.

"As we got those letters, we started doing more tutorials, trying to teach and empower even more. How do you peel garlic? We've done it. How do you cut up a pineapple? You'll find it's actually pretty easy. How do you pick a fresh mango? How do you cook rice? In fact, our most common question is simply how do you cook chicken?" And then Sara adds in a comforting tone, "It's wonderful to be able to really make a difference and help people.

"I really thought the blog was going to be for me, for my benefit. I was going to share how our family loves making cinnamon rolls on Sunday afternoon. I was going to share stories about my mom and her peanut butter and jelly bars. It was her heritage and now that she's disabled, it's a way her legacy can live on. I thought that was what the blog was going to be about. And that's a big part of the blog for me. It's the way I share my life with others.

"But while I'm doing that, the letters continue to come in. Someone learns how to juice citrus. Someone else learns how to use fresh ginger. And someone discovers they love cooking and dinner is once again fun for them and their family. And that,"

Sara adds, "is when I realize my passion helps so many other people along the way."

DARIN-ISM NO. 5

One of the residual benefits of passion is that others can get caught up in the wake and ride along. They can benefit from your passion.

Tiffany Peterson was tailor-made to be a success coach. Her loose reddish-auburn curls perfectly frame her kind smile and reassuring gaze. And her firm, confident voice makes people feel they can succeed in whatever they set out to do. That's what made her segments on TV so engaging. She could take any self-improvement task and make it seem so attainable just with her encouraging words.

Tiffany is a highly successful coach and speaker. Corporations shell out upwards of ten thousand dollars a day to have her come and speak to their groups and get them moving. She commands audiences numbering close to a thousand who hang on her every word, anxious to gain confidence and take success to the next level.

But one Sunday evening in January, Tiffany found herself speaking to a relatively small group of young girls and some of their parents. Pro bono. For free.

"I normally speak to sales executives to help them triple their revenues, Tiffany admits. "I help people increase their sales. I teach sales strategies and success habits. And I do that for high-powered executives and highly motivated sales people. I help people get motivated to pay off credit cards, lose weight, write books, attract a relationship and get married, start a business, gain peace and self-confidence. So that's why this group seemed so different."

There were 75 people in the group, maybe a few more. Most of the young girls were giggling with friends. Some were texting. Others seemed disinterested, but sat there politely nonetheless. "Some of them looked like they were blowing me off. And that's what made me want to impact them even more. I looked out at those girls and wanted to share my passion with them. I wanted to touch them and really affect them. But I felt totally intimidated."

"Here I am, a professional speaker and trainer, used to speaking to ten times the number of people who were there that night, but for some reason, it was a little overwhelming and I felt this added weight. But my passion is speaking and motivating people, so I just dug down and had to rely a little more on my passion to get me through."

A couple months earlier, one of the adult leaders had asked her to speak to the girls and Tiffany immediately knew the message she wanted to share. Self-confidence. It doesn't seem too surprising coming from a beautiful, successful, energetic and commanding person like Tiffany. But Tiffany's history was one that none of the girls would have guessed.

She grew up in a broken home with a single mother struggling to earn enough money to outlast the month. She wore hand-me-down clothes and had to make do with what the family could afford. It was rarely anything nice. And in junior high, she was ridiculed for her looks. "I was this sickly looking thing," she told the group that night. "I wasn't even able to break 100 pounds until I was in high school. And I had this bright red hair, which was made worse by the fact that it was permed. I was this stick-skinny thing walking around with big, poofy red hair. I looked like a strawberry cake pop!"

Of course she was teased. Who could resist teasing the only human cake pop in junior high? Her self-esteem was rock bottom.

And here she stands, reaching out to these young girls. They look very much like she looked at 14-years old. They came from a part of town not known for being affluent. Many of them could have been wearing hand-me-downs, just as she had. She looks into their eyes and thinks, "what would I tell my 14-year-old self?"

The answer is simple. "You are beautiful just the way you are. And life is going to turn out just great." She looks them straight in the eyes and promises them, "You will be wonderful."

This is her passion and you can feel it. Many of those there that night did. Adult leaders came up to her at the conclusion of the meeting and thanked her for her words. "It was wonderful," they said. "It was just what we needed to hear." "I wished I had heard that when I was younger."

There were a few girls who also came up and thanked her for words, offering casual thanks. They had been high energy and giggly. "Thanks," they had giggled. "Yeah, thanks," and then they bubbled off on their way. Their words had been polite, if not truly genuine.

And then Tiffany saw the last girl. She was nondescript in her looks. She was forgettable in her clothing. She was the type who could easily blend in almost anywhere, and likely had done exactly that much of her life. She looked like she could have been Tiffany 20 years earlier, just without the red permed hair.

She finally approached Tiffany and looked her sincerely in the eyes. There was something distinctly different about her. She was sincere.

"Thank you," she offered her gratitude in subdued tones. "What you said tonight was just for me. It changed my life. It was exactly what I needed to hear." And then she leaned forward and gave Tiffany a hug. It was an embrace that was low key but sincere.

And Tiffany hugged back, holding what could have been her 14-year-old self.

Tiffany showed up that evening just thinking that she would be doing what she loved, teaching and sharing with others. In the process of benefitting her own life, she changed someone else's.

It took her awhile to find what she is passionate about. In college, she was sure she wanted to be a teacher with an emphasis in helping special education students, but it just didn't feel like the right fit. She eventually went to work for a training company and felt a little more in tune with her heart. But then she discovered speaking and coaching others to develop their self-esteem. That was when she realized that this was her passion.

Nine months after that chilly January Sunday evening that warmed Tiffany's heart, she sat across a glass round table in our TV studio. She was helping us and our viewers to "find your purpose." It's a topic we felt resonated with many of our viewers.

"Do most people even know what their purpose is?" I asked Tiffany right off the bat.

"That's the challenge," Tiffany responded. "Most people think there's going to be a giant blackboard that is going to drop from the sky that says 'this is your purpose'. But it doesn't happen, and there are so many demands on our life that we get into this feeling of 'overwhelm' and we fail to live a passion-filled life."

"But Dr. Wayne Dyer observed that 'your purpose will be found in service.' That's something that even I struggle with," she confessed. "Sometimes I ask myself what I want to be doing with my life and how I want to be contributing."

And then she pulled out the quote that struck the heart chords of every soul-searching, passion-devoid viewer. "Parker Palmer is an educator and author who put it best. When you find the needs of humanity meeting with what brings you joy, you will find your calling."

Words that reinforced the point, but certainly hearkened back to the lesson that Tiffany was reminded on a cold January Sunday night when she got the chance to use her passion to help others. It was on that night that she did what brought her joy. And it was on that night that she touched a soul and changed a life.

6

The Invitation to Lunch With a Little Brown Bag

Passion is power

One day my boss had an idea. She thought it would be fun to send my co-host Brooke and me to a voice teacher. She wanted us to take a singing lesson and then record a little music. I didn't say it was a great idea.

It was fortunate for us that Dean Kaelin was nearby. Dean is a pseudo-celebrity in the singing lesson world. He had coached dozens of aspiring vocalists, a few of whom had made a name for themselves on *American Idol*. His biggest claim to fame was Season 8 runner up and judges' favorite David Archuleta. The thinking was, if he could turn David Archuleta into the singer he was, he could at least do something with us.

We showed up at his modest studio which he runs out of a small, older home. What was once a quaint 50's bungalow had been turned into a mecca for singing star wannabes. The old plaster walls in the front room were filled with 8x10 glossy photos, CD covers, and yellowing newspaper clippings. The late winter sun streamed through the large window and bounced off the glossy black grand piano. That's where he ran us through some exercises. He did scales that weren't really scales. They jumped all over the place. I thought it was just because he didn't know the scales very well. It turned out, he claims it shakes up your brain and allows your voice to sing in a way you wouldn't normally be able to.

Brooke and I both picked a song to sing. She selected "My Favorite Things" from *The Sound of Music*, and I picked "Hey Soul Sister" by Train, mostly because it had been playing on my iPod just before I got there and it was sort of stuck in my head.

We worked up a little 30-second selection from the song, and after running through it a few times, we went down into what appeared to be a dungeon in the cellar. It turned out, instead, to be a recording studio. Who knew?

Then he started the recording. And as soon as he did, I tensed up. It doesn't matter how much you have practiced or even performed. Once you know it's being recorded, you freak out just a little (some people, a lot). You concentrate intently on the notes and hitting them. You don't want to be sharp. You don't want to be flat. You don't want your vibrato to get out of control. You don't want to slide around on notes. So you let your mind focus on the most important thing there is: hitting the right note.

We ran through the song a time or two, tweaking a thing or two. And then Dean paused everything for a minute.

I stood in the middle of the recording studio, surrounded by all that egg carton foam to absorb the noise. I had my earphones covering one ear and not the other. I had a giant microphone right in front of my face with some high-tech-looking screen thing in front of it. I thought it was to stop food projectiles that might come out of my mouth. It turned out it was to diffuse "popping" sounds that certain words make. My guess is that it would also diffuse a peanut fragment from that Snickers bar inadvertently shooting out of my mouth, in case that happened.

Dean was in another room, separated from us by a giant glass window. He pressed some button so I could hear him through my one-ear-on earphones. He almost seemed to sigh for a minute, as if he were about to say something for the hundredth time.

Quietly, he started, "I don't really care about the notes. Don't worry so much about hitting the right notes."

He didn't care about the notes? He didn't care about the notes? What could he mean by that? He had just run me through the gauntlet singing scales in Hungarian so that I would be able to hit the right notes. Upstairs, with him at the piano, it was all about the notes. And now we descend into the dungeon studio, and he has the nerve to tell me he doesn't care about the notes. What could possibly be more important than the notes?

"What I really need from you," and then he hesitated for just a bit as he focused his gaze on me through the large plate glass pane until he finally urged, "is feeling. It's passion. I can fix the notes. I can make it sound like anything you want. I can make your voice sound perfect. There's one thing I can't do. I can't add the passion. That's what I want to hear."

And so that's what I gave him. I didn't worry about the notes. I sang with no regard to pitch, but with regard to feeling. It didn't sound pretty. But I trusted him.

And when I had finished, I joined him on his side of the glass window. He clicked buttons and pushed slider bars, turned knobs and clicked his mouse. Before long, he had done exactly what he had said. He could fix the pitch problems, and there were plenty of those. But as I listened to the final draft, it had passion. It wasn't just a musical rendition. It was music with a message. It had come alive with feeling. It had power, thanks to passion.

Passion is power. It's often overlooked. We rarely think of it as a tool of power, but it is. When someone is persuasive in an argument, they are using passion as power. When we think of a time we have been motivated to action, it is often because of passion as power.

That power comes across more than you would think.

Producing a daily TV show requires a lot of planning and communication. Once a week, we all get together to talk about the upcoming shows. We have about six of us who are responsible for various segments for each day's episode. Each day, there are about seven varying segments that make up the show. It might be a cooking segment or it might be a fashion demonstration. But the producer who is in charge of that day needs to know exactly what to expect from each element. What is happening during the segment on "Five Ways to Decorate Your Craft Room with Rubber Bands"? What should we expect for "Chicken Manure: Not Just For Compost"? We go through all the segments and make a "pitch" for the segment we are coordinating.

Nothing great was ever achieved without enthusiasm.
~ Emerson

The show producer takes notes so she can know which will be the strongest segments. She quizzes the person in charge of that segment to get an idea of what she has to work with.

It's a conscious effort to gauge the passion of the person in charge of producing that segment. If Jane isn't too fired up about the segment about natural home recipes to get rid of bugs in the garden, then viewers at home surely aren't going to get too fired up about it either. If Angie isn't excited about the new options and trends in stationery, then it clearly isn't something we should be leading with. But if Mallory can hardly wait to share what her guest has discovered when it comes to the new face of wallpaper in home décor, then that segment has some potential. And if Mindy even brings some samples of the new summer water toys that will be unveiled during a segment she's producing, you can feel the passion for it.

A producer, looking for the best potential elements for a show, looks first at the passion of the people involved in it.

On one occasion, we finished up a show and glanced at the rundown for the next day. That's when we noticed something was wrong. We needed a little something extra for the following day. It might seem odd. After all, it's a 60-minute show. How important is two minutes? For Pete's sake, just let some other things run a little long. Oh, if it were only so easy. Instead, we knew that we had to generate a short mini-segment for the show.

The weather had been warming up and we decided to ask two of the guests who were already coming in to just share their favorite picnic idea. It could be a trick for a more enjoyable picnic, a favorite treat to bring along, or some way to forget that you're sitting on hard dirt, eating with your fingers and swatting insects. (Seriously, I've never been a huge fan of picnics. Haven't we evolved to something better than eating on the ground in a way far removed from modern conveniences?)

The show's producer came to Angie who was coordinating one of the two guests. Angie shared that her guest, Alisa was going to talk about clothespins to hold down the tablecloth in a wind. The producer wasn't crazy about the idea. She didn't know how substantial it was. She pushed for more information and wanted to know how good the content was. That's when Angie let loose with a string of "passions."

"Alisa is really passionate about this," Angie started. "She thinks it's a good idea and she can cover the information quickly. She seemed passionate about the clothespins. It's a good idea, and I could sense that she had passion for the idea."

Okay, I'm going to confess that I didn't write down every word she said, so I'm not 100% sure that's a direct quote. But I did count that she said "passion" three times in describing the idea. THREE TIMES! It was a very high ratio of "passion" words to other words. Clearly the message was that Alisa had passion. That was all that needed to be said.

The producer was satisfied, walked away and even moved the segment up higher in the show purely based on Angie's recommendation in regards to passion. The next day, Alisa presented her clothespins with the promised passion. She sang the praises of the idea, and had viewers convinced that they couldn't even think about a picnic without the clothespins.

Another passion of mine has roots in theater. Years ago, a roadshow was a short vaudevillian production. But it has morphed in a mini-musical production, and various groups stage them in a competition type setting. They come across my plate only every three or four years, but when they do, Katie bar the doors, you haven't seen a person obsessed with a passion until you have seen me in "roadshow mode."

One person with passion is better than 40 people merely interested.
- E.M. Forster

Over my lifetime, I have come to love that art form. Just mention the word "roadshow" and my mind starts going a million miles a minute. I love to create the plot, one that can be told completely in less than 20 minutes. I love to write the original songs. Normally that includes a rousing opening number, a comedic specialty number and a tender love song. But what I really love is coming up with the special effect.

I adhere to the belief that if I want to win a roadshow competition, (and goodness knows that's my real motivation) I have to have some kind of show-stopping, jaw-dropping, eye-popping special effect that will take the audience completely by surprise and make them wonder how it was even done.

Keep in mind that we only have five minutes to set the stage, and then often have to pick up and take everything "on the road" and perform the show again at another venue in just a few minutes' time. So you can appreciate what would have to transpire for some of these special effects.

Once we had two people climb into a hot-air balloon basket and then it floated away, off the stage, only to explode a few seconds later.

There was the time we had a working fountain with a special hidden compartment where the villain hid, only to have the fountain explode a few seconds later.

Or there was the statue in the downtown square, where the hidden treasure was concealed. And you guessed it. It exploded.

I kind of like explosions.

But there was also a maple tree which went into overdrive, spraying maple sap all over the cast and audience. There was an enormous, colorful flower garden that wilted on command. Or there was a wizard whose spell backfired turning him into a live pig.

I can dream up the idea, but I have no clue how to carry it off. That's where the power of passion comes in. I have to ask other people, much smarter than I, to pull off the impossible. When I tell them about my vision, the response is invariably something similar to, "That sounds great, but how are you going to do that?"

And my response is invariable something similar to, "I don't know. I have no idea how to pull that off. But I'm sure *you* can figure something out. Will you do it?"

I've asked lots of different people to do lots of different tasks. And I've heard back through the grapevine a similar response. That normally means they say something to *their* wife, who then says something to *my* wife, who then passes it on to me.

"I really didn't want to do this," it starts. "I really should say 'no', but I just couldn't. I don't know why it's so hard to say 'no' to Darin. But I just couldn't do it. I just couldn't say 'no.' "

It would make me feel a little awkward when I would hear that. I didn't want to impose on people. I was just asking for their help achieving something both fun and worthwhile. If it were something they couldn't or didn't want to do, I would assume they would just tell me. But very few people did. Over the years, almost everyone agreed to help out.

I spent years wondering about what it was that caused people to feel they couldn't tell me "no." I came up with a couple different possible reasons. But it never seemed to be a satisfying answer. Then as I began to explore the power of passion, I realized that was exactly it. It wasn't me they couldn't say "no" to. It was the passion.

Had I been missing passion, had I been lackluster in my presentation, had I been lackadaisical in my appeal, it would have been very easy to refuse. But when faced with passion and all the enthusiasm, drive and energy that it carries with it, saying "no" is as futile as stopping a herd of pigs heading for the trough at dinner time. It's useless to even try.

When tackling any task, don't ever overlook one of your most powerful tools.

Don't forget the power of passion.

The most powerful person in the free world is arguably the President of the United States. So I did a little experiment to try to determine the power that comes from passion. And for this highly scientific research I traveled all the way to the kitchen where my wife was whipping up a batch of brownies.

"Honey, I want you to name me the most passionate U.S. Presidents that come to mind."

She cracked the eggs and thought.

"Reagan was passionate." She stirred and thought some more. "Definitely Lincoln. And I think the first Bush wasn't as passionate but George *Dubyah* was." She likes to call him that. "You think about right after the attack on 9-11, he was totally passionate. Oh, and Nixon. I think that he was really passionate. Not always in a good way." And then, just to make sure you didn't think that she was a right-leaning electorate, she added "and FDR. He was very passionate about his programs and getting things done. I'm not saying I agree with them, but he was certainly passionate."

Then, as she was measuring out the cocoa and the dry ingredients, I asked the other side of the coin. "Now who would you pick as a president who was NOT passionate?"

I likely shouldn't have asked that while my wife had a wooden spoon in her hand and was just stirring everything together. As she thought, her stirring became more deliberate and forceful.

Finally, "Carter. He wasn't passionate at all. I mean, sure, he tried to do some good things. But he was just not passionate. And Clinton, the only thing he was passionate about was interns. I guess that would technically make him passionate." By now the batter was being whipped into a frenzy and was almost changing consistency. "Oh, and Ford. I don't even have any strong opinions about him. He had no passion at all!" The stirring continued, at a near fever pitch at this point.

With many recipes, like brownies, if you overmix them, they turn out tough. I felt like I needed to calmly tell her to put the bowl down and step back. Instead, I did something that stopped her dead in her tracks.

"Now which of those presidents were one-term presidents and which were two-term presidents?"

She stopped stirring. She just stared into the air as it sank in. All of her picks for being passionate had been reelected, while the other group was just in for one term.

30 minutes and 350 degrees later, I thought about that over the shoe-leather square disguised as a brownie I gnawed on.

Passion is an immeasurable motivator. It moves individuals. It moves teams. It moves audiences. It moves an entire country.

Passion is power.

The most beautiful makeup for a woman is passion. But cosmetics are easier to buy.

- Yves Saint Laurent

American Fork High School is known for its marching band, the caveman mascot, and a quirky teacher known as Grammar Sam. Sam Beeson is one of those precious commodities of an individual who genuinely loves teaching.

"I like drumming," he told his wife Sarah when she wanted to know his passion. "But that's not it. I really like spending time with my family. But I'm not sure that's even it. In terms of a passion, I really like teaching. That's what my true passion is."

Sam has been teaching since the mid 90's, but there was one epiphany for him when teaching became "absolutely awesome." Most teachers wake up each day and ask what am I going to teach and how am I going to teach it. But then there's another breed of teachers. "Those are the teachers who are going to change the world. And they humbly ask 'Who am I to be given this responsibility?' because they realize that they are the vessel through which the curriculum is going to come."

It sounds a little deep and philosophical for a high school English teacher. But think about any person who has attempted to teach you anything. Sam figures you give yourself about 10 seconds and then you have made a judgment about the person. "Most of us are pretty good. We can nail them down pretty quickly in about ten seconds. You do it consciously or subconsciously, but either way, you evaluate who that person is and what they're about."

That's why we love the monthly Grammar Sam segments on TV. Sam is likeable, genuine, witty, and smart, but not so smart that you feel dumb around him. He has a kind way about him that makes learning seem so approachable. We're not the only ones.

It was about Sam's fifth year of teaching when the *Steve Incident* occurred. On the first day of school, Sam looked up as a large Latino kid walked into his 10th grade English class. This kid was full of bluff and bravado. He was wearing baggy everything. He brandished his cocky attitude as he strolled in and proceeded to jockey for position.

"He was a dingbat," Sam noticed. 'He came in swearing some big time words. Seriously, he hadn't been in the classroom for three minutes and he was swearing."

Sam stepped in, "Excuse me. I don't even know your name. But you're going to have to stop that."

Steve stared him down and swore at him.

Sam tried to play it cool. "Seriously, you're going to have to go out in the hall. We can't have that."

Steve played his profanity card again.

Sam calmly kept at it, telling him he really had to leave the classroom and go out in the hall. Steve finally exited, and didn't return. Steve had a reputation at the school. He was known to be a rebellious kid. He hated school

Steve's sister had had Mr. "Bee" the year before and had loved the experience. And now, Steve was in the class simply because his sister had persuaded him to take Mr. Bee's English class. His first day obviously wasn't as impressive for him as it had been for his sister. Sam wasn't about to let this kid and his disruptive demeanor destroy that class, or his passion for teaching. He knew his passion would have the power to win Steve over.

He tracked Steve down. "Hey Steve," he said later in the hallway. "I sense that you're a passionate kid. But if you're going to stay in my class, you're going to have to do something." He didn't tell him to stop the profanity. He didn't tell him to stop the disruptive behavior. He didn't tell him to be on time, do his homework, or try his best.

"Steve, if you're going to stay in my class, you gotta come to my room and have lunch."

Steve laughed at him. "No seriously," Sam went on. "You're probably a decent guy. I want to get to know you. There will be some other kids in the class. Some of them will be taking tests or doing other things. But I want you to come have lunch with me."

At lunchtime, Sam went down to the cafeteria and bought two little sack lunches. Two little ham sandwiches, two little cartons of milk, with two cups of mixed fruit. He went back to his class and waited. The second hand on that oversized, institutional school clock churned around and around while Sam sat there. He opened his little school lunch and started into his ham sandwich. No Steve. He opened up his cup of fruit and made short work of that. Still, no Steve. He polished off the milk in the milk carton. And still, Steve hadn't appeared. Soon, the lunch period was over and while the one sack lunch had been taken care of, the other brown bag sat there, unopened on Mr. Beeson's desk. Sam didn't touch it. It sat there all day. It sat there all night. When he arrived for school the next day, there was the lonely little sack lunch, just sitting there on the desk.

But during that time, the word had gotten back to Steve. "Steve! How could you stand Mr. Bee up?" "Steve, Mr. Bee waited for you the whole lunch period!" And "Steve, Mr. Bee even bought you a lunch, and you didn't show up?"

When the lunch bell rang on that second day, Sam was in his

classroom when he heard the door open. He looked up to see Steve. Maybe he had been guilted into coming. It could have been his sister. It could have been his friends. It certainly wasn't the enticement of the day-old sandwich and milk which were still sitting there untouched on Mr. Bee's desk.

"He finally came and we just chit-chatted. I just wanted to get to know him, and we talked. We talked every day. For that year, he came to my class for lunch every day."

If you've ever seen the Hollywood version of these stories, like *Mr. Holland's Opus* or *Stand and Deliver* or *To Sir, With Love*, then you think you know the ending. But Steve wasn't the type for Hollywood endings. He wasn't about to respond in the typical screenplay format and buckle down and end up getting straight A's and getting a scholarship to some high-falutin' university.

After the first quarter, Steve got an "F." By the second quarter, he still hadn't passed. After three quarters of the year of having lunch with Mr. Bee, he had pulled his grade up to a "D." It slipped again towards the end of the year. But Sam Beeson wasn't just trying to teach his student English.

"By the end of the year, he was great. We could really talk. Steve would be the enforcer in the class. He would tell people to shut up when I was talking. 'Hey, shut up. Mr. Bee is talking.' He had changed."

"I have a passion to teach. I understand it's a powerful tool. But a passion is only powerful like that when it's founded in truth. I understand I have a talent. I can get people to listen to me. So I have to use that passion to bless other people's lives."

Many years later, Sam was waiting in a voting line on Election Day. As he was waiting his turn, he was startled as he felt himself being lifted into the air. Giant arms had wrapped around him from behind and were hoisting him skyward. As soon as he returned to solid footing, he spun around to find himself face-to-face with Steve. "He was huge. Here was this kid who was now 26 years old. And he had nearly given me a heart attack."

"Steeeve! What's up?"

"Mr. Beeson! You're the best teacher I ever had! I love you so much!"

And there in the lobby of Forbes Elementary School, waiting to cast a ballot, Sam realized just how much power lay in his passion for teaching. It wasn't like it was a super power or anything, but it certainly had the power to transform lives. There, teacher and former student had what Mr. Bee called a wonderful conversation. "We had the best discussion. It was so healthy. Here was this kid who had always been a punk, and just look at him now."

I guess that Hollywood ending just took a few extra years.

DARIN-ISM NO. 6

Sometimes our passions are powerful enoug to transform others. Sometimes they are powerful enough to transform ourselves.

Sometimes our passions are powerful enough to transform others. Sometimes they're powerful enough to transform ourselves.

Melanie Douglass was a meek high school student. That might be putting it lightly. She was a pushover. People ignored her. People walked all over her. She was quiet and overlooked. She was one of the shyest students in her high school. But boldness isn't a requirement for graduation, so she timidly walked across the stage to get her diploma when graduation time came around. And then, she retired to her basement where she quietly waited for the summer to pass.

Melanie was raised in a health-oriented household. Her mother would make "green drinks" long before Hollywood had discovered them. Of course, hers simply consisted of pineapple juice and spinach in a blender. And her mother would send her to school with healthy lunches. That lunch was literally a bag of sprouts. And there were health-conscious magazines around. So it was natural that Melanie was cloistered in her basement during that summer reading a "Health" magazine when she spotted it.

There was an ad for a company called POWER PRODUCTIONS which offered something that caught Melanie's eye: an aerobics music cassette tape. It was music that would get you moving and twisting and jumping. It was designed for fitness instructors to motivate an exercise dance class. But something about it spoke to Melanie. And without questioning it, she sent off for the tape. When she shared her new discovery with family, they laughed at her. When she told friends what she had done, they thought she was crazy. This was meek Melanie who was quiet and shy. How could she ever possibly even consider teaching an aerobics class? She didn't even speak to people. But the tape finally arrived and Melanie quickly retreated with it and a boom box back to the basement.

The basement consisted of a long narrow family room. There was imitation wood paneling on the walls and orange shag carpet on the floors. But the length of the room was more important than the décor. "I could do grapevine dance steps up and down that room all I wanted," Melanie remembers fondly. "And all the while, my family would just make fun of me. They didn't come down to watch. They would just stay upstairs and roll their eyes. It was all just so against my personality. They knew I would never be able to actually get in front of 50 people and teach a class. They looked at me and just said 'Whatever! You can't even speak two words.' But the music is really what changed me. The more I listened to it, the more I opened up and felt I could really do this."

The summer of 1993 wore on and Melanie danced on. From the basement of her home, she started each day as she popped in that tape and was greeted by the pulsating "If you want more, more, more, then jump jump for my love. Jump In!" The Pointer

Sisters were her constant companions as she danced and jumped her way around the room.

"That tape was what catapulted me. It was this fire that got me going. I just started going nuts," she laughs. "The music is really what changed me. It did something to me. It just opened me up like nothing ever had."

After a summer of knee lifts, side steps and Ruth, June, and Anita Pointer, Melanie was as ready as ever. She showed up at The Body Fitness Center and auditioned to teach a class. They spotted her potential, hired her on the spot and gave her a class right away. "Instructors don't start when they're 18. But I did. And I was so nervous. When I popped my tape in and 'Jump' started playing, that music was all I needed. It took over."

Melanie became synonymous with music. She went through a phase with ABBA and Mama Mia. Then there was the Tub Thumping stage. After that, she had an obsession with the Eurodance group 2 Unlimited. She developed a following with her music. Now fitness fans seek her out and attend her classes just because of her great music. Class members ask for her music. Even other instructors do. She's a self-professed music junkie.

When we first invited Melanie to come on TV for fitness segments, we didn't realize the story of her music passion. It slowly leaked out. We would ask her to do a segment on giving your arms a great workout. She would send us her own hand-picked music to play while we were doing the exercises. We wanted a segment on a time saving workout in 10 minutes. She would send more music. We thought a segment on proper walking form would be helpful. She had music for that.

Music for proper walking form? Could she be serious? We found out she was.

She soon started pitching us ideas for segments. How many beats per minute your music should be for a great workout. Where to find the best workout music. Apps to slow down or speed up your workout music.

But while we gave her free-reign with segments on music and exercise, we didn't realize that it went beyond the walls of a fitness room. Mel is a music junkie in countless areas.

Years earlier, she had written her first book, "Losing It: 5 Keys to Successful Weight Loss That Work." Her muse: her music. "I wouldn't dream about doing it without music. The beat is a driver. It helps me stay on a steady pace. The music doesn't distract me. It drives me."

When she developed her own fitness program, *Tonic*, her co-creator was music. "I would listen to hyped up music while I was doing it. It gave me inspiration."

Music is her driver in all areas. On Sunday mornings, when she's wanting to be in a different mood, music gets her there. And when she's cooking, music is on the menu.

And now, that once shy and timid high school student who couldn't say two words to anyone is a movement. She has taught classes around the country. She even presents her ideas to other instructors outside the United States. She speaks to thousands of eager fitness aficionados, packed into ballrooms until there is no more room.

She credits it all to her music. "You just have to have great enthusiasm, and I still get that from my music. Now, I'm just crazy about it." She has even hired her own DJ to create custom music tracks.

Where others might think you need to focus outward, Melanie says it starts inward, with your passion. "I think things have been so successful because I'm doing something that resonates with me. It's something that I find passion with. And only then, can I bring everyone else up, too. It's a powerful tool to have."

"I think I have discovered that music is my passion because it drives me to do whatever I do better."

That seems to be it. Passions are like that little "squared sign" in math. You know, the little two or whatever it is that hangs out on the upper right side of some number to tell you how many times to multiply that number by itself. Two squared becomes four. Four squared becomes sixteen. Sixteen squared becomes... it becomes ... well, my guess is that it's a really big number. Passionate teaching is far more powerful than ordinary teaching. It can change lives. Passionate singing is significantly more powerful than ordinary singing. It can create chart-toppers. Passionate presidents are far more powerful than ordinary presidents. They can get re-elected. (Perhaps, for some, that's what it's all about?)

When we harness our passions, we take advantage of untold potential power. We can change others. We can change ourselves.

7

Bovine Before Daybreak

Passion is success

Not far from where the mighty Ohio River slices along the top of Bluegrass country is where the Kentucky State Fair is held each summer. The fairgrounds are in the heart of Louisville (which is a two-syllable word: LOO-vuhl). It was there that I got my first opportunity for a live, morning feature report.

I woke up well before the sun even thought about cresting the horizon. I met my photographer at the station and headed out to the fairgrounds. This was the kind of job that you can't plan much in advance. You just go where there might be something happening at 5:00 in the morning and hope you can discover something interesting to report on. As we wound through the dark streets on our way, I wondered what my chances would be of discovering something.

We were headed to the animal barn. I guess the hope was that at least the animals would be awake. There was bound to be someone there taking care of a cow or something. I would only have a few minutes after we arrived before I had to quickly find an angle and be ready for the first live "cut-in" for the morning news. As we neared the barn, I was at least buoyed by the fact that there appeared to be lights on in the building. We parked. I quickly darted in.

What I saw floored me. There was so much action taking place, it overwhelmed me. It looked like the North Pole on Christmas Eve, or at least an animal version of that. I had rarely seen so much commotion. The overhead lights were on full-bore. There were dozens and dozens of cows being readied for the day. There were hundreds of people everywhere.

In one stall, a young boy who was clearly still in elementary school was brushing his cow and applying some kind of lotion or dressing to the sides of the cow's belly. I have no idea what it was, but it made the hide look glossy and shiny. (I secretly wondered if they made a version for humans.)

In another stall, a boy barely older than the first had hair clippers out and was meticulously going over the back of his cow. He crisscrossed the clipper pattern like my father-in-law does when he mows the lawn. It didn't look like much hair was being cut, but he was serious about making it all look neat and even.

Next to him was another boy holding a giant aerosol can. He was spraying what looked like a bovine version of Aqua Net on the ball of hair at the end of his cow's tail. He had a complete arsenal of potions and primpings that would make your neighborhood beautician blush.

As I stood there agog, I was almost run over by a young lady and her enormous Holstein or Guernsey or Brown Swiss or whatever it was. She was tugging it down the aisle and I was right in the way. I jumped back only to have a security guard warn me about where I was stepping. Here in the main walkway, there were plenty of the "calling cards" left behind by anxious bovine.

I began chronicling the events at the animal barn each half hour with live shots. I wandered around talking to people and asking them what they were doing. But it was in between those live shots that I was surprised by the stories I discovered.

Not all the stalls had cows. Many of them had tents. In the tents were sleeping bags. In the sleeping bags were sleeping humans. This was an event for the entire family. They were all there, and Mom would get up and start making pancakes while the cows watched on. Eventually, the really young ones (humans, not cows) would roll out of bed and stare sleepily at the action around them. Sometimes, they would crawl back into the sleeping bag to try, uselessly, to go back to sleep.

This was their home. They didn't have some hotel room nearby. They slept with their cows, and with their pigs, and with their sheep. They ate with them. They passed the time with them. For some, they lived too far away to return home each night. But for many, this was just their life. It was what they loved to do. And although it was a challenge to flip Krusteaz pancakes and not have Bossie lean over to grab the pancake batter pitcher, it was their passion.

I followed the early morning cattle train down to what appeared to be a central hub. There was the milking station where the cows were hooked up to milking machines and hundreds and hundreds of gallons of milk were collected. And then, around the corner, the cows were getting their morning shower. The owner would lather them up and then hose them off. That included scrubbing places I've never considered scrubbing. That truly takes passion.

What could possibly make someone uproot their family for the better part of a week and live in a glorified barn? The noise was a steady drone. The close quarters were invasive. The stench was overpowering.

But then I spotted it. I actually spotted several of them. In many of those cattle-stalls-turned-human-living-rooms, there were splashes of blue. Blue ribbons from past fairs decorated their spaces. They were dedicated to what they loved, and it showed in the form of blue ribbons and success. You could tell which of the humans were passionate about what they were doing. You could see it in their eyes. You could see it in their demeanor. You could see it in their blue ribbons.

Passion breeds success. It is a driving force and one of the great factors in determining someone's success in any endeavor.

Those who have passion are more likely to succeed than those without passion.

When your heart speaks, take good notes.
- Judith Campbell

Thomas Edison once lived in Louisville, Kentucky. There is a small museum there in the house where he lived and got some of his ideas. I spent a morning there doing some live reports showing the highlights. That didn't take long. It's a small house.

Edison is noted as being one of the most brilliant minds of his day. He holds patents for over a thousand inventions. He came up with the light bulb, the phonograph, and cement pianos and cabinets. Hey, I didn't say all his inventions were brilliant. But there, in this house where he had spent some time was a quote there attributed to Edison.

"Genius is one percent inspiration and 99 percent perspiration."

With all due respect for the man who invented the electric chair and then used a giant version on an elephant, I would change one word in that quote. "Genius is one percent inspiration and 99 percent passion."

Sure, sure, it doesn't have the same ring to it. But it's true. The idea is that you have to put in a lot of effort to make something work or come up with a creative new idea. I agree wholeheartedly. But true passion is far more valuable than just "work." True passion naturally leads to work. And the kind of action that passion generates is "invested action." It's not simply doing tasks or going through the motions. You can hire someone to do that. It's much harder to hire someone to have passion.

Passion can make things work like few other things can.

There's proof coming out of your iPod earbuds or car stereo speakers or, if you were born before 1960, your Sony Walkman that you still think is cutting edge technology.

DARIN-ISM NO. 7

When you are able to engage your passion, you greatly increase your chances of being wildly successful.

We all know people who think they can sing. I always seem to sit in front of them in church. A small group of local musicians decided to try to help out those aspiring singers who actually might have some potential. They were thinking about coming on TV to share some ideas on how people can hone their vocal skills. The guy in charge, Aaron Edson, had rounded up some friends who had made it to Hollywood Week and beyond on American Idol. They were gearing up to start some workshops to help the next Carrie Underwoods and Reuben Studdards be successful and I was working with them on their TV appearance.

"One of the things those musicians have in common," he pleaded, "is their feeling. They don't just sing notes. They communicate."

"It's all about the passion and the feeling," he said. "Just think of some of the most popular musicians around. Many of them were actually horrible musicians. Have you heard Li'l Wayne sing? He can't! But he gets his message across. Remember Bruce Springsteen? He did his whole free concert in Central Park. And even the mayor of New York admitted that while Springsteen was a great entertainer, he didn't have the greatest voice. Think about it. He sounds like he's gargling with gravel. And the classic example is Louis Armstrong."

Then he started doing this Louis Armstrong impression. "What a wonderful world." It sounded something like a 20-year-old Harley Davidson, missing a muffler. It was dead-on. Then he launched into "Hello Dolly, well, Hello Dolly. It's so nice to

have you back where you belong." Now the Harley was dragging
a cinder block across the asphalt.

"He doesn't have a great vocal tone. All of them are missing
that. But they make up for it with their feeling."

Aaron has this theory about the three levels of
communication. The first level is the written word. That's
someone simply writing down the information. The second level
is speaking that information. That's the spoken word. But the
third level is performing. Somehow, performing and singing
allow for feeling and emotion and passion. And that passion,
when harnessed correctly, can bridge that gap between where we
are and where we want to be.

That doesn't mean that we should all go around singing
everything. It just shows that passion can make up for other
shortcomings and it will increase the chances for success.

People rarely succeed unless they have fun at what they are doing.
- Dale Carnegie

From time to time, on TV, we do something called a "host
chat." It's when the hosts chat about something. (Brilliant idea to
name it "host chat," huh?) More specifically, it's when there is
some topical item or quirky observation we want to tackle. It
might be some new hit TV show. It might be a new store that just
opened up. It might be some new fashion trend.

Host chats can be a gamble. A lot depends on intangibles.
Sometimes, they work and sometimes they don't. You're not
relying on some guest to walk you through some points in a
structured format. It's just the two hosts talking and hoping that a
10 second idea will somehow blossom into a 3 minute segment
that is riveting. We've had plenty that were great and memorable.
And we've had plenty that we wish we had never done.

One day, my co-host Brooke came to work bubbling over with an idea she had for a host chat. It had been Mother's Day and her mom had been given a toy dog. "It's a toy dog that you put on the floor and it rolls back and forth and laughs!" she proclaimed through giggles. "We all sat around and just watched it and laughed all evening." Brooke got some doubtful, blank stares in return.

She left the dog with us while she went about preparing for the show, confident we would see the potential in a laughing dog as a "home-run host chat." We stared at the dog. We poked at the dog. We didn't see much potential in the dog.

But then, Stephanie, the producer, stated the profound. "Brooke has a real passion for the dog. It's our host chat."

And with that, the laughing dog was put on the rundown for a host chat segment at the end of the show. The thought was that if we ran out of time, the laughing dog would never see the light of day.

The end of the show rolled around, and surprisingly enough, we ended up having time for the dog. Brooke pulled it out and explained how she had come to know this dog, and explained how Mother's Day had been dominated with the rolling, laughing dog. Then she set the dog on the table in front of us and the dog did its thing. It looked just the same as it had when we experimented with it before the show on our own. But this time, there was an added element: Brooke's passion. In her voice and eyes and actions, you could see her passion for the dog. Suddenly, the host chat started working. We all started laughing along with the dog. We became infatuated with this little roly-poly beagle giggling his heart out. Viewers loved it, too. They wanted their own little giggle dog. But it wasn't the look of the dog that made it come alive. It wasn't the sound of the laughs that made people fall in love with it. It was Brooke's passion that made the host chat a success and made the dog a star.

Another time, our producer, Michelle, noticed that it was "Name Your Car Day" and wondered if we should do something on that. There were scoffs at the thought. How ridiculous. Who would ever name their car? It didn't seem like something that would resonate with viewers. It would make a horrible "host chat."

Then I spoke up. "Are you kidding me?" I asked incredulously. "You mean you don't name your cars? I have named every one of my cars. There was Gimpy, then Peppy, then Lemonhead. People even stopped and took pictures of themselves with Lemonhead," I interjected with a tinge of melancholy for the old car. I continued, "I've had Legendary Black Max, Peapod the First and Peapod the Second. There was the Bat Truck and now I've got the Platypus and Oldy Goldy Moldy because someone found toxic black mold in the trunk and gave it to me, but it doesn't bother me." I finally stopped when I noticed the scrunched up brows staring back at me.

Clearly none of them ever named their cars. They doubted the potential for the host chat idea. But I protested. "No, I want to do this. Let me lead it. I'm going to do something on naming your cars."

That was all that was needed. They sensed my passion for it. "Name Your Car Day" was put on the rundown.

When October 2 rolled around, I showed pictures of all my old cars and explained what their names were and why. Then we asked viewers to send in stories of their cars and what they had named them. That's when things can get dicey. Either it works and you get lots of response or you get one email from a guy named Booger who is lonely for company.

It worked. We had more responses than we could read.

Kim, a mom of five boys named her minivan "The Monkey Hauler." There was a hand-me-down Camry that Jill had obtained through a series of fortunate events. She felt it was her fate. So the car was named "Karma Camry." People shared how they named their cars after colors, like the white van that became "Vanna White." (Vanna's owner mentioned they were looking for Botox for cars.) Others shared how the license plate letters were their inspiration. That's how "Li'l Eva" got her moniker. And then there was Angie who had cobbled together various parts from the junkyard. She created a mismatched, hodgepodge of a green Ford she named "Frank," short for "Frankenstein."

After the show, we often hold a quick stand-up meeting to evaluate what went well and what could have gone better. Stephanie, the producer for the day, talked about what a fun show it was. "The Name Your Car Day stuff was great. It was much better than I thought it was going to be. And I think it was Darin's passion for the idea that really made it successful."

Passion for rolling, laughing dogs. Passion for cars with names. Passion, we learned, makes elements on TV successful.

Don't ask what the world needs.
Ask what makes you come alive, and go do it. Because what the world needs is people who have come alive.

~ *Howard Thurman*

Boston is full of historical milestones and attractions. While living there, I became amazed at the unique claims to fame they hold.

The first chocolate factory in the United States was in Boston. Tollhouse cookies originated near Boston. And Parker House rolls were created at the Parker House hotel. So there are unique things to eat.

The largest collection of Monet paintings is there. The Granary Burial Grounds are where Thomas Jefferson and Samuel Adams were buried. And just glancing at the outside of the Red Sox's Fenway Park is an experience. So there are unique things to see.

You can climb up the 294 steps in the Bunker Hill monument. You have to take a ride in the swan boats at Boston's Public Gardens. The tours aboard the USS Constitution are "can't miss." I discovered what a plethora of unique claims to fame were there and started working on a simple card game. It was a card game to show off all the things to eat, see and do in Boston.

It took a while to get it perfected. In fact, by the time I had figured it out, I had moved away from Boston and was living in Louisville, Kentucky. That didn't stop me. I just adjusted it to fit the attractions in my new hometown, and I was ready with *EatSeeDo*, a game that was designed to expose tourists to all the unique attractions in any given city. That first prototype was for Louisville.

The plan to finance and get the game to reality was to approach the various attractions and see if they would cover some of the manufacturing costs. My friend, Liz, knew the manager of the downtown Brown Hotel. It was the home to the famous Hot Brown sandwich, an open face turkey, bacon, Hollandaise sauce creation that can make grown men weep. Since the Hot Brown was a unique thing to "eat," it could be part of the game. Liz arranged for me to have a meeting with Brad Walker at the Brown Hotel.

I got dressed in my best business entrepreneurish suit, copied off some great visual images on some super glossy paper, got a nice portfolio folder to hold all the supporting papers and headed downtown to the historic hotel. I sat in the opulent lobby, waiting for the appointed meeting time. I felt out of place watching the high-powered executives and their designer shoes walking past me. There was a little intimidation as I entered this business world where I wasn't acclimated.

Finally, Brad showed up at the appointed time. We exchanged pleasantries and he ushered me into the restaurant in the adjoining room. We sat at a dark wood table that was older than I was and more valuable than my 401K. After chatting a bit, Brad leaned back and asked, "So what is this idea you have?"

That was my cue. I pulled out the pretty pictures. I produced a prototype of the game. I explained the premise of the product.

I had rehearsed my explanation of the game and went through without a hitch. I started dealing out the cards, testing the water to see if he even wanted to go through a quick hand of cards. (He didn't bite.) I explained the rules, which cards can be played when, how quickly the game can be learned, how simply it can be played. I was eager and enthusiastic about the game and how it could be a great venture. Finally, when I felt I had exhausted most of what I could explain about the game, I asked Brad what he thought.

Some people are game people. I sensed Brad was not. At some point during the conversation, I worried that his eyes were glazing over. As I asked for his input, he took a sip from his coffee, put it down and glanced at the cacophony of cards on the table. "This can be a success," he said in a very understated tone. "It's not going to be a success because of this," he said, gesturing to the papers and cards. "But this is something that will be a success because of your passion. This is going to need someone who believes in it and has the passion to see it through. It could work, but the most important thing it needs is passion. And you clearly have that. Your drive and energy and passion will be what makes this successful."

I took it as his blessing. I remembered that edict as I approached tourism officials and tested the water with other businesses. My greatest strength was not my detailed business plan or my manufacturing acumen. It was my passion. Passion was what would make *Eatseedo* a success.

I live in a small town. (Actually, I live in a suburb of the small town.) And when that small town of Kaysville wants to have a town party, they just send out an email asking for help. Who can help with the chili cook-off? Who wants to head up the daddy-daughter dance? Who can be the chairman of the Monster Mash Halloween Dance? Typical small town charm. Now they want their socials to be a success. That's their number one goal. So when they send out the email, they specifically say that people don't have to have experience in event planning. They don't need to have any expertise. But they do require one thing.

"Commitment and passion are what we're looking for."

They might be small town, but they know what makes something a success.

The key for successful TV is to keep things fresh. While we have some regular guests who have a loyal following, we're always looking for new, fresh faces who can bring compelling ideas. One year, we decided to take our search to our viewers.

We staged a contest and asked viewers to videotape themselves doing what they pictured as an ideal TV segment.

It's not enough to have a passion. You have to practice your passion.
-*Kirk Weisler*

I guess there are a lot of people out there who would like to be the next Martha Stewart. Who knew? We were flooded with videos of some of the craftiest people out there. They showed tricks with using freezer paper to make glitter stenciled shirts. They used scrapbook paper to make colorful pennant banners. They turned old discarded books into a witch's cookbook or Santa's "naughty and nice" list. We poured over the videos analyzing them to see who we thought could carry a TV segment with their personality and project.

But we hadn't just asked them to turn in a videotape. We had asked them to tell us a little about themselves. They told about their families. They shared stories about their upbringing. But there was one thing that caught our eye the most. It was when they shared their passions. We even took notice about how many times they used synonyms for the word "passion." It wasn't like we counted up the "passion" words and invited those who used it most. But we analyzed the prospective guests and when we took all things into consideration, the ones who scored the highest in our judgment were the ones who had passionately expressed their interests in word and presentation.

We found some remarkable guests who were able to contribute to the show long after the promotion. They were people who understood that if they wanted to be successful, they needed to let their passions shine through. They did, and they were successful.

It is by acts and not by ideas
that people live.
~ *Anatole France*

Most kids come home from school a little hungry. Some might grab a PB&J. Others might snag an apple. My kids pick up a yogurt. For Amy Richardson, her go-to snack was homemade éclairs. She and her sister would whip up *pate a choux* dough, bake up little puffs and then fill and frost them for their mid-afternoon treat. If it's hard to imagine young pre-teens slow-cooking custard cream for filling éclairs on a Wednesday afternoon, you don't know Amy.

Amy's passion is not just cooking, but being creative. "I just think about all my whole life, whether it's acting in the theater, designing costumes or choreography, or of course, cooking. It's all an expression of creativity. You just get such a fulfillment from creativity."

You might have guessed that Amy has a little background in the theater. Her family ran a community theater in downtown Salt Lake for years. When Amy and her new husband, Owen, moved from Seattle to Salt Lake, she was immediately drawn in by the intoxicating opportunity to be creative.

She designed costumes to transform actresses into human palm trees. "I found this ruffle taffeta fabric that we used to make full body dresses, and then we had these baskets on their heads with ferns coming out." Another time she and Owen created the entire look for "Curious George." "We had the whole thing set in the 40's. It was so stylized and super designed. Owen painted all the scenery so it looked as if you were stepping right into the book."

While she was putting all her creative efforts into the theater, she would occasionally hearken back to her éclair roots. But she was now in a cookie phase. She would create over-the-top cookies and bring them to share with cast members. She created Black Forest Cookies with three kinds of chocolate and dried cherries and Apricot White Chocolate cookies (you can probably figure out what's in that one). She became famous for her fun, unexpected treats.

So it was only natural for her name to come up when the Bar Mitzvah event popped up on the calendar. Some theater patrons wanted to do something special for their son's bar mitzvah. Guests would be flying in from around the country and the hosts wanted to impress. They rented out the theater for a private performance. And with the entertainment taken care of, they just needed to figure out the after-theater dessert. Amy's name immediately rose to the top of their contact list.

It was her first foray into something like this. Sure, she had made her creative cookies, but those were trivial compared to what she was now being asked to do. The order was for 40 different cakes to be served up after the performance. And not just any cakes. They had to be 40 different ones. They had to be 40 unique ones. They had to be 40 creative ones.

Since they had to be fresh, Amy was going to have to complete this task in the 24 hours leading up to the event. She mapped out the plan of attack with baking and decorating timed down to the minute. She even bought 20 Springform pans to accommodate her baking schedule. "I still have all those pans down in my basement 20 years later," she confesses.

And then, with the clock ticking down, Amy sprang into action. She made a hazelnut mousse torte. There was a strawberry mousse cake. Black and white cheesecake. Black Forest cheesecake. Triple chocolate cheesecake. Triple raspberry mousse cake with white chocolate mousse. Banana Fosters cheesecake. Orange and tangerine mousse cake.

Amy lives in an older, character-filled home in the historic part of town. But when those homes were being built a hundred years ago, they never dreamed of someone making 40 different full-sized cakes, so the kitchen got a little cramped. "I had cakes everywhere. They were all over the kitchen. They were all over the living room. They were all over the house. I had them at my Mom and Dad's house next door. I had them at the neighbor's. I took some down to the theater as they were being finished. Most of them had to be refrigerated, so I found whatever available fridge space there was in the neighborhood and took advantage of it. Rounding them all up and taking them down to the theater was an ordeal. It took several trips to get them all down there." Amy's cakes were the hit of the evening. Guests couldn't get enough of them. The loved the variety. They loved the flavors. The loved the creativity. "There were all these people from Chicago and New York and they loved it. They loved all my cakes. I could probably have started a business from that one night alone. I had all these people coming up to me wanting to know if I could ship cakes to them back east."

She had been on a 36-hour adrenalin high by the time the party was winding down and the big-city guests with their big-city tastes were wandering out of the party. Amy sat there and basked in the glow of what had just happened. "Even though I had done lots of other creative things, this was one of the first times I had done something creative with food. And it was totally fun."

It was an eye-opening experience for her. She had certainly experienced lots of success being creative on the stage, but this was uniquely her own. She wasn't working with her husband. She wasn't working with a cast. She wasn't working with a technical crew. It was just Amy and her passion together in the kitchen.

When we had a last-second cooking guest cancellation, one of our producers thought of her neighbor, Amy. "I don't know how she would do on TV," Maeve confessed, "but her food is amazing and she's always making creative things."

Amy accepted our invitation to come cook and she served up her passion in the form of a Margarita mousse that you could use three ways. You could serve it plain, with fresh berries in a parfait, or in a crust for a light summery pie. It was novel and refreshing to see her passion in a cooking segment. And we invited her back again and again. She became one of our favorite contributors because of her genuine love for cooking and our genuine love for her creations.

2010 was dubbed the Year of the Foodie for Studio 5. The foodie trend had been building and appeared to be coming to a peak with magazines, blogs, TV shows and overall buzz centered around food. We wanted to launch a special feature that year to ride the foodie craze. And we needed the right guest to be our "Gourmet Today" contributor. It wasn't just about food. It wasn't just about gourmet trends. It was about creativity and Amy's passion for that fit the bill. It was an easy decision to have her be the face of the new "Gourmet Today" franchise.

I wanted to give her the news in person, so I stopped off on my way home from work. I set up the concept and then blurted out, "And we want you to be the new Gourmet Today contributor!"

She was a little overwhelmed at first. She stood there in the entry of her home and thought about what it would entail, the time commitment, the pressure, the expectations. Glancing at Owen, she said that she would have to think about it.

But over the next few days, she thought about something else: the creativity. This was the perfect way to unleash and foster her passion for creativity. There would still be a time commitment and pressure and expectations. But those weren't anything new. Those things had all been there on the afternoon of the 40 cakes. She would take care of her passion, and those things would take care of themselves.

Amy splashed onto the scene with her "gourmet today" creations. With the "gourmet" banner nudging her, she became even more creative than before.

Chicken burgers with fresh oranges, avocado and lime mayo.

Blackberry chipotle pulled pork with dessert hand pies.

Key lime, white chocolate and spicy ginger ice cream with spicy pepper ginger cookies.

Butterscotch hot wings.

Gourmet grilled s'mores with flavors like white chocolate apples and cinnamon, Key lime pie, and dark chocolate and raspberry.

Roasted chicken and sweet cherry spread on a croissant.

Fruit sushi with sweet jasmine rice and assorted fruits.

Dessert wontons with white chocolate and pear, banana coconut with a caramel dipping sauce, or marzipan filled with a raspberry sauce.

As our "foodie" year ended, so did some of the other "foodie features" we had introduced. But not Amy and her "Gourmet Today" moniker. It was so successful that a local grocery store stepped in to sponsor the segment each week. They went on to print her weekly creations on recipe cards and distribute them in all their stores. It is one of the most successful ventures we have launched.

Amy's passion for creativity had made it a success. "The creating of something is so much fun. I'm thinking, 'Oh my gosh, why didn't I think of that.' There's such a joy in creativity. That's where we find happiness."

"Sometimes people don't like it when you are passionate. It makes some people nervous. It makes them crazy. But there's some kind of energy that comes from it. There's so much happiness to be found in being creative. And we have such a small smidgen of it in our pathetic lives. Why not embrace it and do something with it?"

Creativity is where Amy finds happiness because it's her passion. We each can find that happiness in our passions. And when we do, just as Amy did, we find success.

Whether you're raising bovines, or baking cheesecakes, whether you are proposing a business idea or performing in front of an audience, there is a key element. When you are able to engage your passion, you greatly increase your chances of being wildly successful.

8

Gingerbread Garlands In A Golden Kitchen

Passion is Life

Christmas in the 70's looked a little different. The 70's were the decade of brown and gold.

The Bedell home was a modest one in quaint Centerville, Utah. It had dark wood cabinets with gold countertops. The flooring was brown linoleum with a big square tile pattern. The appliances were a lovely harvest gold. And draped around the kitchen was a brown statement, which made the most impact in the room.

The Bedell family had made dozens of gingerbread men cookies. They were wrapped in plastic wrap and then strung together in a wonderful ribbon that ringed around the room. There was a steady stream of visitors to the Bedell home at Christmas, perhaps to visit with the family, but more likely because any guest got to cut down his own gingerbread cookie to eat.

It was in this home that Alisa Bedell Bangerter grew up. Alisa, now grown with a kitchen of her own, has a passion for parties and decorating and food and making people feel like there's always something special happening. Alisa is one of the most anticipated guests we have on TV. She brings her passion with her every time she is on and is unabashed in her enthusiasm for what she does.

"My passion?" she paused for a second. "I love decorating. I love holidays. I love parties. Whenever I get to the store, I'm always wondering what I can do with things I discover. I don't know why I love it so much, but I do!"

Think of Alisa as a Martha Stewart with passion. Don't get me wrong. Martha is a creative genius. But she's always a little understated. It's almost like she's afraid her chickens will laugh at her if she gets too excited. Not so with Alisa.

She's always been that way. It was in that wonderfully brown-and-gold kitchen that Alisa has some of her first memories of celebrating holidays.

"It was warm in there," she recalls, remembering both the temperature and the emotions. "My mom was always cooking. She taught me. She was awesome. It seems as if we were always making something."

Christmas was a quest to have as many presents as possible. She would cut pictures out of magazines and make cards with them. Sometimes the magazine picture actually *was* the present. Then she would wrap everything she could find. She would scour her room for little trinkets that could pass as presents. She would even find things that couldn't pass as presents. And then the wrapping began. She wanted to fill the holiday with all the gifts she could. Then the organizing would begin. She would pull out all the presents from under the tree and spread them all over the floor. Then she began piecing them together like a giant puzzle, fitting present up against present until all the boxes formed a giant wall-to-wall replacement for the gold shag carpet. As more presents appeared closer to Christmas, it was a new challenge everyday to re-work her gift organizing process. But every day, she pulled the presents out and started anew, like a giant crossword puzzle on the floor. (Even as a newlywed, she admits to wanting as many gift boxes as possible. She would wrap completely empty boxes in coordinating wrapping paper, just for the look of a tree packed with pretty packages.) Then as Easter approached, she would organize the egg hiding and hunting. She would kick off the egg hunting games with her younger brother and two younger sisters. What was odd was that she would start about a month before Easter ever rolled around. It would start with all the plastic eggs. It wasn't the pursuit of jelly beans or malted milk eggs. It was simply for the fun of the holiday. She would hide them for her younger siblings and then they, in turn, would hide them for each other. With about two weeks to go until Easter, the real eggs came out. The family would dye dozens of eggs and then take turns hiding them. By about this time, the parents were involved in the hunts. Parents would hide for kids. Kids would hide for parents. It was just the fun of hiding and finding. Alisa does confess that there was more than one occasion when the hiders were better than the finders. "We would try and try to find some of those eggs, but some of them were just too well hidden and we never found them. Then, sure enough, since they were hard-boiled eggs, we would start to smell them. It would be a long time after, but pretty soon, they started stinking. At least that helped us to find them."

The family celebrated Valentine's Day by putting envelopes on the headboards of all the beds. Gifts would magically appear in the envelopes. Or they would find their shoes mysteriously filled with gifts.

They would distribute flower baskets to friends on May Day. They would come up with crazy Halloween costumes. They even made up holidays just to have an excuse to make a batch of cupcakes and hand them out to anyone who wanted to celebrate.

She would take plastic lids off of containers and spend afternoons making homemade "shrinky dink" crafts.

There's even a photo somewhere of Alisa positioned on the kitchen counter, standing directly in a pile of bread dough. She had seen her mom kneading dough for some project and Alisa figured she would give it a try. No one had told her she couldn't do it with her bare feet.

"It gets in your blood. You just get excited. There's something about all the holidays, the parties, the food. It's just magical."

Then Alisa got into high school. "They used to call me...," she pauses, not sure if she's ready to divulge her past. "Betty Crocker," she finally blurts out. She's quick to point out that she wasn't a nerd, by any means. She was popular. She was head cheerleader. She was prom queen. But everyone called her "Betty." At the Senior Banquet, she was voted "Most Likely to be Betty Crocker." (In reality, there probably wasn't much competition for a title like that.)

She started entering cooking contests. She won. She tried convincing others of her happiness and her newly discovered source of cash prizes. No one seemed eager to give her any competition. No one dared compete with "Betty."

Decades later, Alisa has become arguably the foremost authority on creative parties and holiday festivities in a state that prides itself on its family traditions and celebrations. When we run a check on which TV segments have been viewed the most over any given past year, there is always an Alisa Bangerter segment in the top 5.

"I don't know why I like it so much," she admits. "But I do. I just love all that holiday stuff. Sometimes the anticipation of the holidays is actually more exciting that the holidays themselves. It's the build-up with all the sights and sounds that you create. It's like putting a warm blanket around you."

When I asked Alisa which was her favorite segment she has done on TV, there was a long pause. Then she started pulling up old computer files while rummaging through a big file cabinet packed with handouts and patterns and ideas and outlines, all categorized by year. She was quiet as she poured over the years trying to recall which was her favorite.

Finally, after what seemed like an eternal silence, punctuated only by sounds of thinking and reflecting, the answers started coming.

"I really like the Halloween table décor. That was great. I got to have blood on the drinking glasses, but not too gory.

"Perhaps it was that cake decorating segment. Or it could have been the cupcake decorating one. That was fun.

"The creative things to do with fall leaves. I had to come up with some new stuff for that one.

"Oh, wait. The fun things to do with Chinese culture. That was when the Olympics were in China and I really had to do some research on that one.

"I enjoyed the Twilight movie segment, but that one probably shouldn't count.

"I loved the fudge one. We had all the different flavors of fudge for a Christmas fudge buffet bar.

"Oh gosh, it was fun to do that one with my mom. That was on the family reunion ideas.

"I liked the one with ribbon, all the things to do with ribbon.

"The cookie cutter one. Creative things to do with cookie cutters and how to make your own cookie cutters.

"The chocolate transfer sheets. We showed people what they were and how you could use them to make some impressive desserts that look like they are so professional."

I got the idea it was like I was asking her to pick a favorite child. The choices were clearly too numerous and every one made her excited. "It's ridiculous," she laughed. "It really is. It becomes a part of you. It's just these things you love."

Alisa's passion for parties serves a two-fold purpose. She views it as a pseudo-family insurance policy. She'll have you think back on most of your childhood memories and then she's quick to point out that about 80% of them revolve around holidays and parties. Those traditions link your family together for generations.

But her passion does *her* good, too. It gives her drive a core and connection. It gives her direction a fix and focus. It gives her a love of life.

"I know I'm passionate when I dream about things. I wake up with ideas that I just have to write down in a notebook. In your free time, when you're just thinking about stuff, your passions are the things that you just naturally think about.

For Alisa, it's gingerbread garlands and fudge buffets.

DARIN-ISM NO. 8

Passions aren't the magical fountain of youth. Pursusing them is.

There's just something that happens in your mind and your body when you are doing something you love. There's an energy and life that pulses through you. Alisa certainly knows that. It's part of what keeps drawing her back to holidays and parties. Those who engage in their passion know the excitement and anticipation that builds before. They know the rush of happiness and adrenalin that happens during. They know the joy and release of stress that happens after.

It's not just a psychological benefit, but a physical benefit. Studies show that people who are engaged in activities they love are not just happier, but healthier, too. The happiness is not just a selfish reward, but goes beyond that. Want to make more money? Want to be more productive at work? Want a more satisfying marriage? Want more friends? Want to be healthier with lower stress levels, less pain and a better immune system? It all comes down to doing something that makes you happy. The happiness doesn't always come *from* all those things. The happiness can lead *to* those things. And doing what you love, pursuing your passion, leads to true happiness like little else.

In 1934, little Mihaly Csikszentmihalyi was born in what was then Fiume, Italy (now Rijeka, Croatia). The family was Hungarian, but Mihaly's father was part of the diplomatic corps assigned to Italy. World War II was the horrific background for Mihaly's early life. One brother was killed, another was taken prisoner and sent to a labor camp in Siberia. Even Mihaly was held for a time in an Italian prison camp.

While the situation around him had deteriorated, Mihaly tried to find some escape. He found it in a strange place, on a checkered board surrounded by castles and bishops. It was chess. He found it was a miraculous way of entering a different world where nothing else mattered. When he entered the world of chess, he left his other world behind. In the world of chess, there were clear rules and goals. "If you knew what to do, you could survive there," he realized.

The art of being happy lies in the power of extracting happiness from common things.
~ *Henry Ward Beecher*

It was his first exposure to what can happen when you immerse yourself in a passion. You can lose yourself and enter a new realm of happiness and focus. Years later, he met other Hungarians who had been part of the gulag prison system during the war. Some were psychologically destroyed while some seemed at peace, and almost happy. He was intrigued by the discovery and came to a hopeful idea, based on chess and Hungarian prisoners. You can create your own happiness.

He was fascinated by psychology and came to America to study at the University of Chicago. He studied how adults organized their thinking and how it sometimes went horribly awry. He learned from some of the psychoanalysts and forward thinkers of the time as he tried to figure out a better way to organize his thinking and order his life.

And so, in the 1980's, he had an idea. He handed out beepers to high school students. He would randomly contact them throughout the day and ask them how they were feeling right at that moment. Like typical high school students, they reported they were unhappy most of the time. Maybe they were feeling tied up learning Newton's laws in physics class. Maybe they were dropping a batch of curly fries at the Burger Barn. Maybe they were waiting for Dreamy McHunksville to ask them to the prom. There's a lot of teen-aged angst to make you feel unhappy. Their persistent unhappiness wasn't a surprise, but their occasional happiness was what piqued his curiosity. Sprinkled in between all the locker drama and unrequited relationships, there were moments when these students actually were happy. It was when they were focused. It was when they were doing something they were interested in. It was when they were challenged.

Csikszentmihalyi became fascinated first with adolescents and then with all humankind, and what made them happy. He discovered that we are happiest when we are doing things that are challenging and centered on activities that mean something to us. It has nothing to do with being selfish and ego driven. He created the word, "autotelic" which means an activity done for its own sake.

It might be easier to describe "autotelic" for what it's not. It's not an activity that gives us external rewards. It's not something we do to get fame or fortune. It's not something that solely gives us power or comfort.

Instead, it's something that gives us an inner reward. We do it because we love it or have a deep desire to do it. A teacher isn't going to get independently wealthy teaching first graders how to read, but she gets a reward when she hears them plowing ahead into a difficult book. A scientist or researcher might not be close to winning the Nobel Prize, but takes comfort in knowing he could be getting close to helping others improve their quality of life. A religious counselor isn't going to get a new Ferrari from working with a couple struggling in their relationship, but does it sincerely because he is making a difference and saving a family.

Those are examples of autotelic activities. Csikszentmihalyi might have come close to calling them passions. And when we are engaged in them, we, like the high school students, are happier.

Csikszentmihalyi then took it to the next step to analyze exactly what happens in people's hearts and heads. He interviewed athletes and artists, scientists and scholars, the teachers and the "teachees." They all had experienced the joy

and focus that Csickszentmihalyi was seeking. They often described their experience as similar to being in a river. From that, Csickszentmihalyi came up with his theories of "flow."
He came up with a collection of different factors that often accompany "flow." There are specific and challenging goals. There is direct and immediate feedback. Intense concentration is involved. In return, the person becomes absorbed into the activity. He might lose track of time. And it can even lead to a lack of awareness of bodily needs such as eating or sleeping.
Legend has it that Michelangelo painted the Sistine Chapel while he was in a state of "flow." The masterpiece ceiling at the Vatican was the perfect challenge that enveloped the artist. Supposedly, he would paint for hours on end without stopping for anything. As hours stretched into days, he would eventually simply collapse from hunger and fatigue. After a while, he would regain awareness, feel refreshed, and jump right back into the "flow."

The work you do while you procrastinate is probably the work you should be doing the rest of your life.

- Jessica Hische

Flow is similar to what athletes describe as being "in the zone." The basketball hoop seems larger than normal. The golf hole seems huge. The baseball seems like a giant beach ball just waiting to be hit.
When I met former San Francisco quarterback Joe Montana, he was about 20 years removed from one of his greatest "flow" days. The day I interviewed "Comeback Joe" he was promoting heart health and showing me how to make a healthier version of potato skins. We were in the kitchen scooping out the innards of halved baked potatoes and dressing them up with the appropriate

fixin's. He was still gracious and cool under the hot studio lights, but I can remember one of the more memorable times I saw him in action.

I had been a 49er fan growing up and 1989 was one of their greatest seasons. They made it to the Super Bowl against the Cincinnati Bengals. While Joe had played brilliantly, the prospects of victory seemed dim for the 49ers. They were losing 16-13 with only 3:20 left to go. And they were backed up on their own 8-yard line. While a field goal could tie it, he really needed a touchdown to win, a touchdown that seemed an impossible 92 yards away. But that's when he took to the field and entered what must have been a state of "flow." He rifled off nine passes and completed eight of them. He marched the team a stunning 97 yards with a near-flawless performance that was capped off by a beautiful touchdown pass to John Taylor with 34 seconds to spare.

He was in focus. He was in the zone. He was in a state of flow. Was it a challenge? Certainly, and one that forced him to rise to the occasion. Was it one that brought immediate rewards or feedback? There's nothing like seeing them move the chains, realizing that end zone is getting closer and closer. Was he not aware of bodily needs? I'll bet he never once thought about needing to get a chug of Gatorade or grabbing a Snickers bar. Okay, so it was only a few minutes. Most of us could go that long without Gatorade or a Snickers bar. But you get the idea.

Tell me, what is it you plan to do with your one wild and precious life?

~ Mary Oliver

Most of us will never play in a Super Bowl or paint the ceiling of a chapel. But we have other passions that can usher us into a state of flow, or at least bliss. These states not only make us happy, but studies show that they can actually promote better health and well-being. Barbara Fredrickson has been sending people to the movies for years to prove just that. She is a social psychologist at the University of North Carolina and is out to prove that happiness leads to health. She had a group watch movies that encouraged positive emotion. This group laughed and seemed content while watching the movie. The second group saw movies that produced negative emotions. They were scared or sad. Then another group saw movies that produced no emotions. (There is no truth to the rumor that they used Weekend at Bernies 2, Gigli, and any Alvin and the Chipmunks film as the movies for this test group.)

The group that saw the "positive emotion" films showed greater creativity and inventiveness. They had better "big picture" perceptual focus. Those people with more positive feelings are shown to have greater resilience and flourishing skills. And it's not just because they didn't have to watch Weekend at Bernies 2, Gigli, and any Alvin and the Chipmunks film.

It makes more sense to think that negative emotions are a better motivator. It's the old "fight or flight" that kicks in. It's what preserved our forefathers when they were fighting off a saber-toothed tiger. It saved the lives of our "knights in shining armor" ancestors who jousted and dueled for their lives. It's what gave old Great-great-Granny the gumption to pick up a skillet and whack it upside the head of intruders to her cabin on the Great Plains. That's the negative motivator. What good could possibly come from positive motivators?

Fredrickson says "plenty." She argues that it's the positive motivators that served them best. It allowed them to broaden their minds. It fostered a desire to think. It encouraged them to build the social resources that would mentally get them through hard times ahead. It was those positive emotions that gave them the fuel to keep going when their surroundings seemed to spiral out of control. It was those "good" feelings that gave them strength to get through the "bad" times.

Now picture you're that "hunter" forefather of ours and you've just encountered a herd of wooly mammoths on a stampede and you're right in their path. It's a narrow trail with a cliff leading up on one side and a ravine leading down on the other. Your negative emotions start kicking in. Your palms start sweating and your head gets dizzy (signs of stress). Your heart is pounding and is working as hard as it can to ramp up the strength to outrun the mammoths (increased heart rate and elevated blood pressure). Your body starts accessing stores of energy to fuel the sprint along the cliffside trail (increased blood sugar). And your nose starts twitching as you feel a cold coming on (immunosuppression). Granted, that nose-twitching thing is likely to be the least of your concerns.

Those are some of the negative health concerns that come about from negative emotions. You're going to die earlier. But compare that with the "gatherer" forefather who is on some hillside enjoying picking fresh gooseberries and mint leaves to make a refreshing summer drink. He's basking in positive emotions and is far healthier. It's not just that he's healthier because the mammoths trampled the first guy. It's that research shows the positive emotions help him manage stress and get back to his physiological baseline. And he doesn't even know he has a physiological baseline.

"Phooey!" you say as you read this. Happiness never got anyone anywhere. That gooseberry picking Neanderthal is never going to get anywhere in life. It's the other guy, the hunter, who is going to get ahead. He's tough. He's strong. He's rugged. He's going to be the one to succeed. He has faced the wooly mammoths and will come out ahead.

First, we don't even know if he's going to make it out of the cliffside showdown. And second, his stress is going to get him nothing but an early grave (provided he survives the wooly mammoths).

Happiness, something we figure the "gatherer guy" is experiencing, has great benefits. Flash forward, away from the gooseberry patch, and right into your life. Think of something you do that causes happiness. (That could be pursuing your passion.)

Benefits of happiness include greater work productivity and better quality of work. Throw in higher income levels and it's a slam-dunk. Those people who are engaged in happiness activities (read passions) have happier, more satisfying marriages, and their marriages last longer, too. They have greater social lives with more friends and stronger social support. They have better health thanks to improved immune systems and lower stress levels.

And finally, happy people live longer.

"Gooseberry guy" was going to live longer than "wooly mammoth guy." Who knows, maybe "mammoth guy" was a MacGuyver type from 100,000 years ago and his passion was hunting down wild woolies. If so, then he's pursuing his passion and he just leveled the playing field (as much as you can when your passion is hunting down wild, crazed animals that weigh eight tons).

I'm so tired of people needing a reason
for doing everything in their lives.
Do it because you want to. Because it's
fun. Because it makes you happy!

- Unknown

If you're happy and you know it, clap your hands because you are going to live a longer, healthier and more social life than if you weren't happy. Passions are the magical fountain of youth. Check that, *pursuing your* passions is the magical fountain of youth.

Monster, Red Bull, Rockstar, and 5-hour Energy all have something in common. When I was young, we just used trail mix or Gatorade. But now, it seems that everyone has some product designed to give you more energy. It is such a "buzz worthy" topic that we devoted a whole month to finding energy. Licensed Clinical and Social Worker Julie De Azevedo Hanks had been studying many of the people she helps in her practice and we were anxious to find out what she discovered. Her discovery surprised me.

"You have to have passions," she revealed as we sat around the glass table reflecting the bright studio lights. "Passions are the key to getting more energy."

It had nothing to do with getting a massage or going for a walk or even taking a nap. It revolved around passions.

Julie gets lots of people who come to see her about getting their life properly aligned and getting to a happier place. "I have these people who are coming in to my office who have simply lost touch with their passions. These are the things we care deeply about. Passions are a way to know why we're on the planet."

While she sees passion deprivation among all cross sections, she sees it most with women. Here are women who have silenced what they love, what they care deeply about, in the name of "being a good mom." It's all done in the service of their kids, but somehow, they lose track of who they are. They lose track of themselves.

"The irony is that they sacrifice their true self, who they really are, to be who they think they need to be. They don't realize that being in touch with their passions will actually make them better people in all their roles. It allows you to be closer to other people. It gives you more to share. You're a better mom when you are in touch with your passions."

Julie conducts workshops where one of the main accomplishments is to get people back in touch with what they love in life. These are people who don't know what they're doing, they aren't sure where they're going. "So one of the first things I do is ask them what brought them pure joy as a child. Kids are easily joyful and passionate about their life. It's a great indicator of what their passions might be."

For Julie, it's where she discovered her passions.

As far back as Julie can remember, there was always a big Steinway grand piano in her home while she was growing up. Her father, Lex, was a professional musician and it was his instrument. For Julie, it was her source of joy. She loved singing and having her dad play the piano for her. "He was a human karaoke for me. I would request songs, and he would play them. Music was just a pure joy for me."

Her dad would dim the lights and pick her up to stand on the bench. He would play. She would sing. "Here I was, this little, itty-bitty kid, singing away in this dimly lit room that was like my own stage. I felt pure joy." They were songs she heard on the radio. They were songs she learned in church. She drank it all in, and then, in her dimly lit mock studio with her dad at her side, her passion came spilling out.

As a young pre-schooler, she felt the first seeds of her passion. "I discovered that was one of the reasons I'm on the planet."

She has fond memories of writing songs with her dad. It started as simple poems, and then gradually morphed into her first documented composition, "If You Want to Be Right, Then Don't Fight." It's not likely to make the Top 20 of any music countdown, but it was another step in her passion pursuit.

Back in the 70s, her parents were astute enough to grab a tape recorder and movie camera to record some of her early singing. She has since gone on to record ten albums and earn a number of honors and accolades. It's something that, instead of taking away from her other responsibilities, adds to them. It gives her the energy and life to do everything else even better.

"I was just saying to a friend that I didn't know being a grown-up would be so fun. Over the years, I have simply honored my passions and it has opened up doors for me. It's given me opportunities. It's added to my life. It has helped me to balance being the person I am with all the other things I do: wife, business owner, mother and everything else. And with that, she pauses, "the things I care about define me as an individual."

It sounds easy, but it's hard to do. It sometimes means you have to pursue things that might seem selfish. You have to set aside things that other people perceive as the most important to pursue something that your heart perceives as the most important.

"That's especially hard for women who are the primary caretakers for their families. It's painful to honor both the individual self and the family caretaker," Julie points out. But all too often, she sees what happens when people "honor" just the latter. In her role as musician, she knows what passions can do for her. But it's in her role as licensed clinical social worker she knows what passions can do for others.

She sees people come in all the time who have lost track of their passions. That can contribute to depression. "We make this transition to adulthood or married life, and you have to sacrifice," she is quick to add. "That's just part of it. Every relationship requires it. But the problem arises when you give up everything for another person. That can be a very bad experience. I see people all the time who somehow lost their passions along the way. Maybe they grew up in a family where their individual development wasn't nurtured. Maybe they didn't get the support they needed. Maybe there was a loss or a trauma that got in the way. Somehow they lost it. And they find themselves in a sad or scary place."

But then something lights a spark within them as they begin the journey back. They find their passion. "I've seen it," there's an energy in Julie's voice as she gets to this part. "There's this hope. There's an excitement. There's this beautiful unfolding that I get to see.

"I keep coming back to this one word: vibrance. It's an energy as they discover their passions. They're more alive. They're more excited. They're stronger."

When it comes to some magical secret to happiness, longevity, health and focus, look no further than your passions. Passions are more powerful than potions or pills. Forget the Prozac. Try the passion.

9

The Mystery of the Vanishing Vinaigrette

Finding your Passion

Razor-sharp knives rock back and forth across pecans. Industrial grade mixers whirl whipping cream into fluffy peaks. And the room bustles with energy as chefs clad in white coats glide from station to station assembling a gourmet meal that would rival any 5-star restaurant. But this is no restaurant. It's tucked down some dark hallways in an otherwise deserted high school. The other students have long since boarded buses and headed home. But here, well after hours, Diane Cluff supervises her best and brightest students as they gear up for a high school competition unlike others you have seen. Food Network meets a high school *Intro to Foods* class.

I was assigned to cover Diane's foods class as part of a special look at how Home Ec classes have changed over the years. Diane's classes have perhaps changed the most. She grooms her top students each year for the Pro Start competition, a nationwide showdown where a team of four students creates an impressive meal, and then executes it under the scrutiny of demanding judges. In the previous 10 years, Diane's teams have won the state competition a startling six times, placing repeatedly in the nation's top teams.

"People always say that I'm the most competitive teacher in the state," Diane confesses sheepishly. "But I don't feel that I'm competitive. I'm passionate! The other day, I was at a Chinese restaurant with some other Foods teachers and I opened up my fortune cookie, and it said 'Don't be afraid of competition.' I loved it. And another teacher took the fortune and framed it and wrote 'Passion' underneath it." Her framed "passion" quote now hangs in her classroom as this year's foursome of Tom, Matt, Caroline and Dylan caramelize Granny Smith apples rehearsing their dessert for one last time before they head off to the Pro Start National competition. And here, well after normal school hours, Diane excitedly flits from station to station giving last minute tips and posing questions that a "floor judge" might toss their way during the showdown.

For those who knew Diane growing up, they would find it hard to picture her back in a classroom. School wasn't her forte. She struggled in math. She didn't enjoy science. Many of the academic areas were a challenge for her. That all changed in 9th grade in Los Amigos High School in Fountain Valley, California. There, Diane discovered her passion. "I was so lucky I had Mrs. Haskin that year. I got excited about the cooking and sewing part of class. We called it Home Ec back then. And I loved it. I asked her how she became a Home Ec teacher. She became my mentor and encouraged me. She told me I wouldn't have to worry about math or science and she nudged me in the right direction."

Her grades were not what they needed to be to get accepted into college, but she was able to get in on probation. Her enthusiasm started building as she started taking classes. The idea of going to school seemed more exciting than it had been in a long time. But before she could get too far along, reality hit.

"I was told that I would actually have to take math and science classes after all. But at that point it didn't matter. I was so passionate about my Home Ec classes that I was going to find a way to accomplish the math and science part. I got tutors and other people to help me get through those classes. I loved the Home Ec classes so much that I did whatever I needed to do to complete the program. It was a five-year program that I finished in four years. I took a class in teaching Home Ec and I got an "A" in it. But the teacher told me that I would never make it. She told me that I didn't have the personality for it and I wasn't friendly enough. It was fun because four years later, I was able to go back to her to show her the award I had received for being the *Teacher of the Year* for the state. I just had to let her know."

Now, decades later, the team of Tom, Matt, Caroline and Dylan were getting ready to take their place as the latest in the line of Cluff protégés, with perhaps the best training and preparation of all her teams. Diane has taught them, professional chefs have mentored them, and they have rehearsed their recipes and routines dozens of times. Everything they will need for the national competition must be packed ahead of time and brought with them. They have a checklist of utensils, cookware, and ingredients they have gone over with a fine tooth comb. So with Mrs. Cluff reading off the list, the students check, double-check, and triple-check one last time as they make their final packing preparations.

It's a warm spring afternoon in Overland Park, Kansas. The Pro Start team takes center stage and with a team of judges watching their every move, they begin what they have done so many times before. Tom plays up his showmanship as he whips his egg whites into fluffy stiff peaks and holds the bowl upside down over his head to show the perfect consistency. Matt starts assembling the arugula and watermelon radish for the salad. Dylan and Caroline are launching into the lamb chops with a pomegranate-balsamic reduction.

Tom is responsible for starting the berry mousse that will top the deep-fried apple blackberry pastry with lavender candy. He is searching the ingredients when his heart sinks. A guest observer notices his change in demeanor and alerts the mentoring chef. It takes him just a second to recognize there is a problem. He dashes to Diane to deliver the news, "Something's wrong. Tom is missing something. He's looking all over, but he's missing it."

The adults could only watch and worry. Tom, on the other hand, had no such luxury. With judges scrutinizing his every move, he had to do something. The cream for the vanilla panna cotta was missing and he wasn't sure what he could do.

At that same time, Matt was scouring the work area for a specific bowl. In his laser-focus search for the bowl, and with the pressure of the moment, he casually picked up the aged sherry vinaigrette for the artisan salad and, without even realizing it, he tossed it out.

Months of creating and cooking, practicing and prepping had just been tossed aside because of the missing cream and salad dressing. Diane can only watch, knowing that something is wrong, but clueless about what it is and helpless to do anything.

"It's not the first time that someone has made a mistake in the kitchen," she muses. "Sure, it's a big stage, but it happens. I had a student who was supposed to make *40-Clove Garlic Chicken* and before I knew what was happening, she had cut up 40 entire bulbs or heads of garlic. She thought that whole bulb was a single clove!" She tosses her head back and laughs as she remembers. "There was the other group of kids that wanted to make lettuce wraps and they were supposed to figure it out on their own. They didn't have a clue how to make a lettuce wrap, but they knew that the filling was hot, so they wrapped up the meat in a lettuce leaf and put the whole thing under the broiler, hoping that would magically heat up the filling without ruining the lettuce. Of course, they cooked the lettuce."

"I love to see the bumps and the rough things along the way. Some boys tried to make cookies at home and they came to me and said, 'Cluff, what went wrong? These cookies taste like tuna fish. What happened?' As it turned out, they used the baking soda that was in the fridge absorbing odors, so the cookies ended up tasting like all the bad odors that had been in there."

"I discovered my passion isn't just food. It's teaching kids skills. I don't have food processors in class. The kids are the food processors. I want to give kids tools, teach them techniques. The kids learn the hard way. I've seen them measure the salt over the bowl and spill too much. Then they whisper, 'Keep Cluff busy.

Keep her distracted.' They try to add other ingredients to make up for it. It doesn't work. But I don't care if they make a mistake, as long as they can identify it and correct it."

The *40-Clove Garlic Chicken* girl is a testament to that. Lindsay Kinateder went from cutting 40 bulbs of garlic to receiving a scholarship at one of the most prestigious culinary schools in the nation where she earned three degrees, and is currently the executive chef for a large international corporation overseeing all of Asia. The young lady in her mid-20s clearly learned from her initial garlic faux pas.

But neither Lindsay nor Diane is much help to Tom who is still scouring the work area for any sign of the missing cream and Matt who is searching for the vinaigrette, which, unbeknownst to him, is lying at the bottom of a garbage can. The macadamia nut crusted goat cheese log is just sitting on the salad plate waiting to be dressed. Waiting in vain. But it's then that Diane's passion pays off. Her passion isn't teaching how to follow a recipe. It's teaching skills that will allow you to identify what has happened and fix it.

Tom had salvaged "about one-eighth of a tablespoon of cream" and began whipping it like nobody's business. He acted like nothing was amiss. The team's captain, Caroline, sprang to the rescue. She had saved a few extra berries from the filled pastry and she blended them with the scant amount of cream. She stretched it into something that could faintly resemble a whipped berry mousse. Caroline's expertise was quenelles. A quenelle is a delicate football-shaped garnish that can be very difficult to master. It involves an intricate technique of scooping the mixture with a specialized spoon. You dip and scoop, then quickly turn the spoon back the other way as you lift it and gently lay it on the target. In this case, the target was an unassuming square of vanilla bean panna cotta. Caroline had practiced the quenelle technique for months. And now, with hardly any cream in her mixture, she had to give her best quenelle attempt using heavy berry sludge. But drawing on the passion of Mrs. Cluff, Caroline dipped, flipped, and gently laid her makeshift quenelle on the creamy Madagascar vanilla panna cotta cube.

At the other end of the work area, Dylan leapt to the rescue of the missing salad dressing. She remembered she had a small amount of olive oil left over. She grabbed what was left of a lemon and whisked the oil together with what juice she could wring out of the lemon. It wasn't at all the dressing that had been planned. But she salted and seasoned it into being something passable, and she dressed the artisan greens on the plate just as the judges came by to observe.

The team didn't finish in the top five. In spite of the rave reviews from the judges on the flavor of the foods, they could tell it wasn't exactly what had been planned. And although Mrs. Cluff was disappointed, as was the entire team, she was also enthused by what she saw.

"They were amazing, how they could figure out what had gone wrong, and be creative, and fix it. I love it when I teach students something and then they go and do it better than I would. I feel, 'Wow, that's cool' and to me, that's my adrenalin rush. I'm not perfect, but I'm good at sharing what I have with others, and then seeing what they can do with it. I love my kids. I love my job. I love my foods. I love what I do. "

As much as she would love to have her kids come home with a Pro Start National Championship, that's not her real passion. "I just love it when they can share my spark, my love for it. If they take that, they know they can do it."

Never let the odds keep you from doing what you know in your heart you were meant to do.

- H. Jackson Brown, Jr.

There are infomercials for just about every kind of workout imaginable. But when our TV staff saw an infomercial for hula hooping your way to health, we just had to look into it. I mean, how many calories can you really burn doing a hula hoop? I guess the first challenge is actually being able to do the hula hoop. My skill level consists of simply throwing the hula hoop around me as hard as I can so that it makes at least a revolution or two before it gradually starts losing speed and comes slowly spiraling downward to my ankles, in spite of my best efforts to swivel my hips as rapidly as possible.

The hula hooping fitness craze was a small microcosm of the health realm, but one that we wanted to check into. So we tracked down a woman who actually taught classes in hula hooping. Sheryl McGlochlin had some secrets to successful hooping. She used heavier tubing that allowed you to create your own hoop, and she even filled the tubing with water. She claimed it somehow helped with the "flow" of the hooping activity.

I was doubtful, given my past failures with hula-hoops. But during the segment, Sheryl was somehow able to teach me to successfully hoop for more than five rotations. The hoop kept going. And Sheryl kept cheering me on with this infectious enthusiasm that made me think the hoop was my new best friend.

We loved Sheryl's energy and passion during the segment, and asked if there were any other topics she might be able to cover. As it turned out, Sheryl was not merely a "hooper." She called herself an outdoor enthusiast, but we soon learned that she was simply an enthusiast.

She loved the outdoors and took groups on hikes and trips and excursions around the region. Her specialty was the back country and she knew all the canyons and crannies like the back of her hand. We asked her to come back to do a segment on the "Top 5 Fall Color Hikes" in the area. Sheryl set to work on narrowing her list down to five. She found photos of them and dug up little known facts and returned to our studio one day in mid-October.

We weren't sure how captivating it would be to talk about going for a hike. So to give the segment a little more "setting," we moved outside the studio to our plaza set. Off in the distance behind us, you could catch a glimpse of the color-dappled mountains. Sitting on stools, we rolled some video of beautiful colors and then introduced Sheryl as the outdoor enthusiast who was going to reveal her five favorite hikes to enjoy the fall colors.

"The first one is Stewart Falls," I started off. "Tell us about Stewart Falls."

Sheryl could hardly contain herself. "Stewart Falls! Ahhh!" That exclamation was part awe and part excitement. "It is…" she started and then had a hard time describing the beauty. Finally, she gushed, "You're not going to believe this. Everyone should see this! Stewart Falls is the next best thing to being in Switzerland. It's stunning. The mountains. The colors. The scenery."

Some photos of Stewart Falls were on the screen for home viewers and Sheryl caught a glimpse of them on the monitor. "That!" she screamed, pointing to the image on the screen. "That's the waterfall! It's amazing."

Brooke and I instinctively whipped our heads around, not wanting to miss what clearly had to be one of the great natural wonders of the world. What might have been merely a nice waterfall at any other time, suddenly, through Sheryl's eyes seemed like something wondrous.

We caught our breath and moved to the next one. I wasn't sure how anything else could compare after our initial discovery of Stewart Falls. But we had promised five hikes, so we had to move on to the others.

"What about Stairs Gulch?" Brooke went on.

"Stairs Gulch! Stairs Gulch!" Sheryl repeated with even more enthusiasm than Stewart Falls had received. "Oh, I LOVE Stairs Gulch! It truly is one of my favorites. And the colors. Oh, the colors. You won't believe the colors. There are pinks and purples and…"

She stopped herself realizing that she might have gotten too excited about Stairs Gulch. "Oops. What am I saying? There aren't any purples. But there ARE amazing colors. The yellows and all sorts of colors. The colors are unbelievable."

She went on about Stairs Gulch as if she were telling tales to two toddlers hanging on her every word. We were enthralled about the hike and being drawn into her color-filled world. Eventually, we had to move on to the next one.

"You have discovered some great trails up by the Snowbasin ski resort," I started. "What should we look for up there?"

We should have been prepared for the response.

"Snowbasin! It's amazing! It's incredible! It's absolutely beautiful!" She went on to describe how breathtakingly spectacular the colors were up near Snowbasin.

It's said that not everything can be a superlative. If everything is described as "the best" or "the most colorful" or "the most amazing," then it takes away from all of it. But somehow, no one had told that to Sheryl. Purely because of her passion for each one of the hikes, we believed that each one was beyond comprehension. And she wasn't simply spinning tales. She had photos of the colors from each of the trails. And every time the photos would appear on the screen, she would point and rave about how rich and wonderful the colors were. And each time, we would stare at the screen along with her, and nod our heads, that, "yes, indeed those were the most amazing and vibrant fall colors."

As she wrapped up her list, she gushed one more time. "You HAVE to see these colors. We have some of the best scenery in the whole country right here in our backyards. You HAVE to see these!"

Sheryl's passion is what we love about her. Few of us have actually taken her advice and gone on any of the hikes, but we so want to when we listen to her. We can just feel her enthusiasm and love listening to her excitement.

We have given Sheryl several more assignments. The best hikes with hidden secrets. The best waterfall hikes. The best 30-minute hikes. The best treasures at state parks. And every time, Sheryl shows up with her patented passion.

"Oh, this is my favorite hike! I LOVE this hike! This has really got to be the best hike." We joke that every time we mention another hike, it's going to be her favorite. And every time we do, it *is*. But strangely enough, we believe her.

DARIN-ISM NO. 9

Thinking about your skills calms the mind, but thinking about your passions quickens the heart.

People can find their passions in all sorts of ways, and with all sorts of motivation. For Becky Low, it was a desire to not have to do the dishes. At least that's what her younger sisters will have you believe.

Becky is one of the regular cooking guests with whom I have made countless recipes. And Becky's sisters get partial credit for her discovering her passion for food. Becky was the oldest girl in a family of six children. The two younger girls, Nina and Patty would constantly squabble over whose turn it was to clear the table and wash the dishes. So "Mamma Low" made the rule that if you didn't help fix the food, you had to help wash the dishes. "Of all the rules that my Mom ever instituted, that was probably my favorite one," Becky confesses. And it was the rule that started the races. "My sisters claim that I would run home from school every day just so I would be able to start cooking and then wouldn't have to wash the dishes. But in reality, I think they just liked to play outside. I think they were a little harebrained. But one of my favorite things was after dinner, I could go in and watch TV and listen to Nina and Patty in there washing dishes."

It might have started as just a way to get out of washing dishes, but Becky learned early that she loved cooking food. It was the center of everything good. When her family would sit down for dinner, it was more than just nutrition for the body. It was nutrition for the soul. "I appreciated the time we spent together. I appreciated the caring. I learned to serve and help others. I learned lessons from my mom. We both shared the same common goal. Food was something much more than just food."

Becky knew her passion was working with food, and graduated from college prepared to teach Foods and Home Ec classes in school. But one of her first positions was anything but typical. This was not your average high school job, teaching muffins and snickerdoodles to bright-eyed suburban girls.

Becky headed out to Caliente, Nevada. It is a couple hours' drive northeast of Las Vegas, just a stone's throw across the border from Utah, and scarcely more than a blip along the Great Basin Highway that meanders aimlessly through the desert. Caliente is home to tumbleweeds, jagged rock outcroppings and what was then called the Nevada Girls Training Center. The NGTC was a school for incarcerated young ladies who had made some poor decisions.

"They were there for various reasons," Becky remembers. "Some were there for grand theft, others for drugs, there were run-aways, some had been abused, and others were abusers. Some were there for murder. Of course, not any while I was there," she's quick to reassure.

And there, in the middle of the desert, in a small home economics class, Becky had a class of ten young ladies, many of whom had never been taught what she had grown up practicing. "I saw another side of life there. When someone cares for you, you develop a bond there. You develop a love for children and vice versa. When I was growing up, it was a comfortable feeling when we would sit down for dinner. And these young ladies had never experienced that. They had never experienced what I had experienced sitting down as a family and enjoying a meal together and feeling the comfort that comes from it."

And then in walked Joanie. The best Becky can remember, Joanie was a run-away. It could have had something to do with the fact that Joanie didn't have any complete legs or arms. Her arms stopped at her elbows and her legs stopped at her knees.

She had prosthetics for her legs and hooks for arms. "And if she didn't have her hooks on, she couldn't put her legs on. So she would just run like crazy around the school on her half legs with her half arms swinging back and forth. She could get around like you wouldn't believe."

But what really impressed Becky were Joanie's cooking skills. When she had her hooks on, she could handle knives and pots and pans. When she didn't have her hooks on, she had taught herself how to knead bread. She had caught onto something she could do, and do well. "It inspired me. I had a brand-new focus while I was here at the school. Here was Joanie who had grown up not having any idea what her choices were. She came from a different background and I suddenly saw her discovering what she could do."

"I knew I had a passion for food. I knew I wanted to cook and do something in Home Ec. I knew I had loved it for years. But it was while I was in Caliente, as I watched Joanie, that I started to see why. It was during that time that I realized the power of food and what I could do to help people learn how their lives can change because of it."

I have no special talents. I am only passionately curious.
~ *Albert Einstein*

The magic question in TV is "What do people want to see?" If you can figure out the answer to that, TV programming executives everywhere will worship you. Who would have guessed that viewers wanted to watch B-list celebrities do ballroom dancing as part of an elimination competition? But you make that assumption, and you're the brilliant creator of "Dancing With the Stars." Who would have guessed you could send an FBI agent to some remote town where, by night he has dreams of dancing little people who speak backwards, and by day he praises the town's coffee and pie. That would have been "Twin Peaks," which had a big cult following during its heyday. Or who would have created the most unlovable character in TV: a doctor with the worst bedside manner, a staff that despises him, and a limp to go along with it. That would be "House," one of the biggest medical dramas of its time. If you could somehow figure out the crystal ball of TV programming, you would be set for life.

And to take a gander into that crystal ball, TV stations pay huge amounts of money. It's all under the name of research. They staff rows of phone banks to call and ask people what they like. It's a simple question. And then, we get those answers in the forms of pie charts and statistics.

From that information, we try to make sure that we are helping viewers with their areas of interests. For example, one of the greatest areas of interest is photography. The "mom-tographer" is a big trend and we present segments on how to get great lighting at home, or where the best-colored walls are to stage your family portraits. Gardening is another big response. We schedule segments on landscaping with fruit bushes or the top five new flowers for the season. A lot of our viewers are anxious to find new places to eat out. So we wrangle a dining critic to recommend the best al fresco dining spots, or the most authentic pizza joints.

We're basically asking people what they love, what they're interested in, what they're passionate about. But something happens when I ask people point blank what their passion is.

There is one overwhelming answer that pops up more than any other. "What's your passion?" is the question. The answer: I don't know. Sometimes it's preceded by, "Huh? I don't know." Or there's, "What's my passion? I don't know." Maybe even a, "What's that? I don't have a clue."

Short answer: people don't know. They haven't thought about it. It hasn't crossed their minds. They go about their regular day's activities without even trying to nail down what it is that gets them excited. But before you get too judgmental, if someone had walked up to you a week or two ago and asked you the same

question, you likely would have stammered a "What's my what?
I don't know." I know I was like that until one afternoon when I
had an interesting conversation with one of the most captivating
men around.

Dan Clark has inspired half the world. Maybe it just seems
that way. He has contributed to pretty much all of the "Chicken
Soup for the Soul" book series. He has traveled overseas to
embolden our military troops. He has been in the locker rooms of
Super Bowl football teams firing them up and motivating them
to victory. If anyone knows how to help someone find their
passion, it's Dan.

Dan sat next to me at a table at an afternoon gathering. Soon,
the conversation turned, as it frequently does with Dan, to
passions.

"You have to find your passion," he urged with his rich deep
voice tinged with a bit of a rasp. "What would you wake up at
4:00 AM to do? What would you drive for three hours to tell
someone, not because someone was paying you, but just for
free? If you only had half an hour to talk to someone, what
would you want to talk about? What gets you so excited that you
love to talk to other people about it?"

Since Dan's life revolves around talking, his "passion
questions" tended to center around talking about passions. But it
could also translate to acting on those passions and not just
talking about them.

I have talked to thousands of people and asked them all the
same question. What's your passion?

I am initially met with that same blank stare. It's okay. I'm
used to it by now. But then I start pulling out the prompts. What
gets you excited? What gets adrenalin rushing in you at the mere
thought of something? What gives you butterflies and the
"tinglies"? What gets you so excited you stay awake at night?
What gives you that feeling that makes you think the restroom is
calling?

My wife gets that feeling when she's decorating for the
holidays or throwing a party. My mother gets tingly with the

mere thought of spending time with grandkids. My mother-in-law would wake up early just to garden in our yard.

One lady I met said she woke up in the middle of the night with an idea for a gluten-free bread recipe and she had to finally just get up and start baking. She knew she would never be able to get back to sleep once she got that excited. Another woman discovered her passion was solving mysteries. Her husband took her to a mystery theater and she was so excited, it took her several days of excitement before she finally was able to get a good night's sleep. Someone else told me their passion was laughter, anything associated with laughter. Another person confided that they were passionate about the brainstorming process. They liked the creative, collaborative problem solving process.

What you are in love with,
what seizes your imagination,
will affect everything.
It will decide what gets you out of
bed in the morning, what you do
with your evenings, how you spend
your weekends, what you read,
who you know, what breaks your heart,
and what amazes you.
Fall in love, stay in love,
and it will decide everything.
- Pedro Arupe

The passions I have heard, from musical theatre to astronomy, from church to smoothies, from trying anything new to tracking down family history, never cease to amaze me, but never really shock me. I'm amazed at the diversity. But after hearing so many, I've learned that there are about as many different passions as there are people who will answer the question.

As time wears on, we sometimes forget about passions. They get shoved to the side to make room for other demands. We get caught up in the "have to do" things of everyday life. And there's not much room for passions there. Before long, we can barely remember the days of our passions, let alone determine what our passions still are.

So wake up your passions. Shake off their rust. Discover what excitement keeps you up at night. Uncover what gives you butterflies.

Passions have great benefits; benefits that can only be claimed when we know what those passions are.

10

Lil Wayne vs. Big Pappi

Passion Pyramids

The middle-aged woman finally raised her hand.

I could tell she had been thinking about it for a while, and had finally gotten the courage to ask a question.

This was a special conference on building strong families and I had been asked to conduct a session on how a family that loves and fosters passions is a stronger and more successful family.

I had rallied the parents to climb on board the "passion wagon" and was just about to send them on their way, when the woman in question raised her hand. I quickly called on her.

She smoothed out her carefully-knotted silk scarf. As she rose, she cleared her throat while never breaking eye contact with me.

"What if your child doesn't have any passions?" she asked sincerely. "What if you have an older child who just doesn't think he has any passions?"

My heart saddened for a moment for this poor woman. She appeared to be a wonderful mother who wanted the best for her children, but I got a glimpse into her life for just a second. It might not have been her actual life, but it was a facsimile, which could have replicated her life that I pieced together in a few milliseconds.

I pictured a 20-year-old (give or take a few years) young man who didn't have any direction. He probably spent a chunk of his day sleeping, playing video games or watching YouTube clips online. I'm not opposed to those activities in limited doses, but really? How many times can you watch Charlie biting a finger or check out an annoying orange talking to other produce?

She wanted her son to experience the same joy and happiness she had in her life, but he seemed to think that he wasn't interested in anything. She had come to the conference trying to find some hope or direction. And this was my moment to help her and her son, in just some small way.

"Everyone has passions," I boldly stated to her, emphasizing the word "everyone" as much as I could. "Everyone! The problem is that we get distracted or forget what we love. It's still there, but other things cover it up. Your son has a passion. He just needs to remember it or discover it.

"Just ask him which he likes better between a couple things. Keep doing that until you have a few things that he clearly likes more than others. Then, surround him with opportunities to be part of those activities and see if that can't nudge him into doing things that will get him off the couch and into his passion. Have him do an informal version of the Passion Pyramid."

The Passion Pyramid is a little tool that came from an attempt to keep my kids entertained. We were in a place where I needed them to be subdued and quiet and they were getting a little antsy and noisy.

It must have been around March and the NCAA basketball tournament was on my mind. So I quickly pulled out a piece of paper and sketched a modified tournament bracket, and penciled in some of the favorite people of that particular child. Sponge Bob Squarepants and Miley Cyrus made the list. Another list included Tiger Woods and Tom Brady. When I had filled out the bracket, I handed one to each child and let them whittle away at their favorite people. Lil Wayne beat out Big Pappi and moved on to face Wee Man. The Teletubbies got run down by Thomas the Tank Engine, who revved his engine against Lightning McQueen. For each list, one by one, the contenders fell by the wayside until there was just one remaining. That last champion was that child's favorite pop culture hero at the time.

The bracket exercise served two purposes. It gave me a glimpse into what captured my kids' imagination and attention. It kept them quiet for 15 minutes.

When I first started coaching people in discovering and engaging their passions, I was surprised at the number of people who had no clue what they were passionate about. Their passions had somehow gotten lost in daily life. So what worked for keeping my kids quiet could help those people.

DARIN-ISN NO. 10

Wake up your passions. Shake off their rust. Uncover what gives you butterflies.

Time after time, I have pulled out the bracket I call the Passion Pyramid. In the eight openings at one end of the horizontal pyramid, you list activities that you really enjoy. Then you pit one against the other with the winner advancing to the right. Which one gets you most excited between the two? Which one gives you a thrill? If you had your choice between doing one of the two, which one would you pick? Your favorites do battle, round after round, until one emerges victorious. That is your passion.

There's not a science to this. It's just a way to help people see there are some things that they are passionate about.

It's an exercise I have carried out with thousands of people. Frankly, I have been a little surprised at some of the top passions that people have shared. Needlepoint would never get me excited. Nor would poetry. But they were top passions for some. Astrology was another passion that caught me off guard. And I never would have even thought to include "Mystery Dinner Theater," but one woman did and she discovered it was her top passion.

So that's the tool I told the middle-aged woman at the conference to try. If her son wasn't about to get off the couch to play croquet with the family or take a hike, he likely wasn't about to fill out a Passion Pyramid. But she could stealthily fill it in for him and get an indication of what might be the motivation to help him pursue his passion.

And then, you just need to do it. Don't wait for motivation to get you involved. On some occasions, actions will lead to motivation. But someone who has lost his or her passion is going to have a hard time getting the ball rolling. Instead of letting motivation move you to action, start with the action. It will reawaken the passion and lead to a natural motivation. If it doesn't, then it's likely not the right passion. Go back to the list, and try again. You won't be penalized for getting the wrong one. But you will eventually be rewarded when you find the right one.

I've included a few Passion Pyramids in the book. You likely will only have to do it once. But you can let others try it. I had my parents fill out the first part, and then I tried to guess which passions would win. For my wife, I was even so bold as to fill out the first eight activities and then predict the final outcome. (I nailed it.)

And if you run out of pages, let's face it. It's not the most complicated form to replicate. Draw some lines on a piece of paper and give it a try.

Let the Passion Pyramid point you in the right direction.

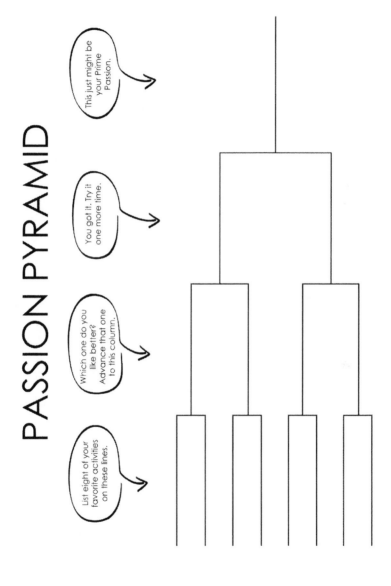

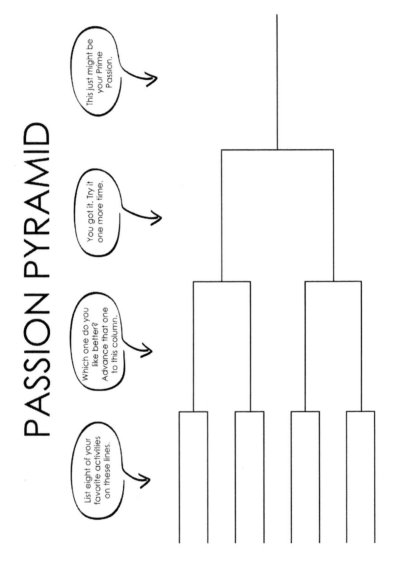

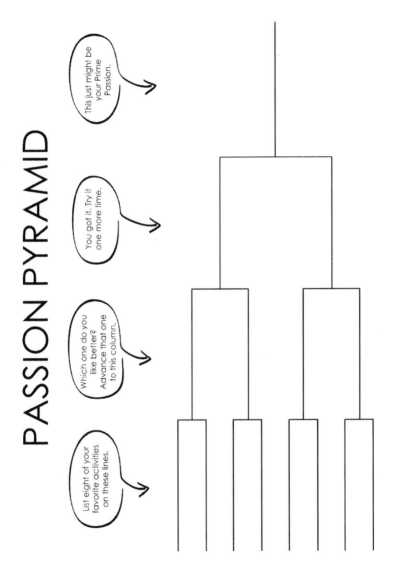

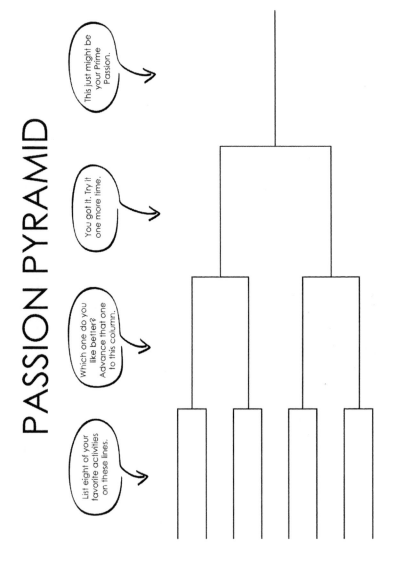

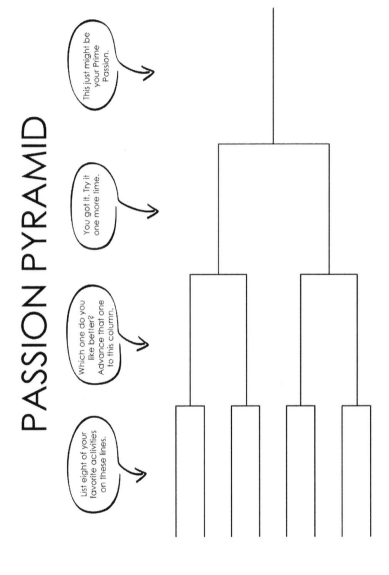

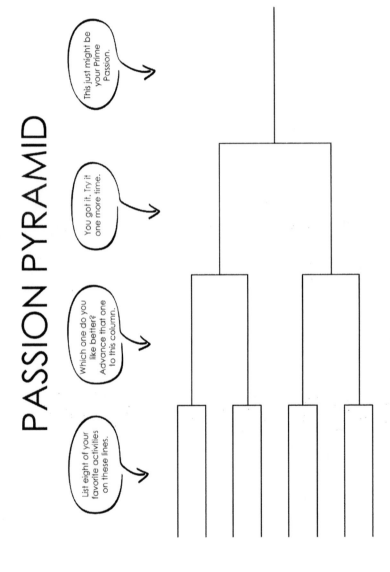

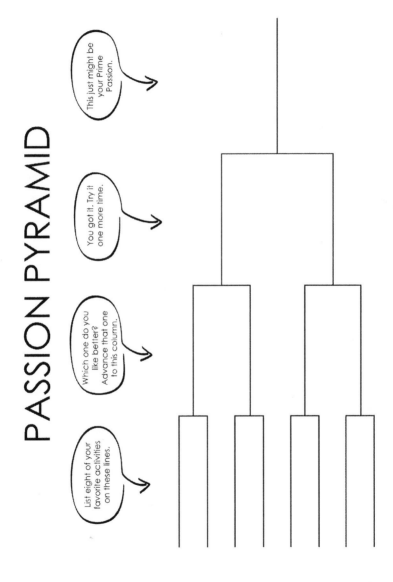

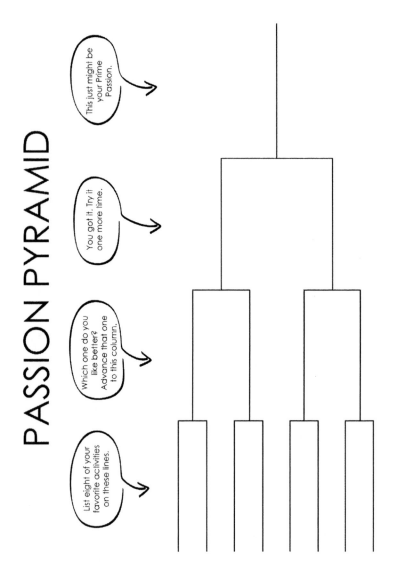

11

What's Really Inside the Violin Case?

Finding time for your Passion

The violin case of Jenny Oaks Baker is a sight.

It's worn and tattered with frayed edges and faded coverings. But the real treat is inside. As you lift the lid of the case, there is the smell of wood that's older than anyone you have ever met. There is the glint of a polished bow that has been twisted and turned in untold ways. You can almost hear the tone and timbre of the treasured instrument.

As the case opens, you can see some elastic cords that stretch across the inside of the upper cover. Tucked inside these are icons of her passions. She has crumpled sheet music, stained and yellowed. Surrounding those are family photos of her husband and four children. Two passions that symbolize the struggle that happens daily with a violinist the likes of Jenny Oaks Baker.

For seven years, Jenny was a first chair violinist with the National Symphony Orchestra. It is generally recognized as one of today's finest orchestras, situated in the nation's capital. Jenny fit perfectly as one of the nation's most celebrated violinists.

She had released 8 previous CDs and now her 9th one had just come out. "Then Sings My Soul" had catapulted to No. 1 on Billboard's classical charts. Famed cellist Yo-Yo Ma had been knocked out of the #1 spot thanks to Jenny more than doubling his sales. Luciano Pavarotti was clear down at No. 11.

We had scheduled Jenny for a live performance just as she was having unprecedented success. Before we let her pick up a bow, we wanted to find out how to do it. How can you have a passion as time consuming as "professional violinist" and still be the loving and devoted mother that you want to be?

"Passion needs to be a priority," Jenny said through a contagious smile and sparkling eyes. "I'm a better mother because of the passion I have in my life. I think if you find something that helps your soul to sing, you can be happier in your existence. I encourage men and women to find something that makes them come alive and have that as a small part of their lives."

Regardless of the accolades that come her way because of her musical prowess, Jenny's real passion is being a great mother and wife to the five other people in her home. That's what she loves to do. It's an altruistic passion that she loves as she can see the positive influence she has in their lives. But she also has that other passion. That's the one that she carries in that worn and frayed violin case. She has to find time for that one.

Her older kids are musical and she spends the day with them, making sure they get their practicing done. "At the end of the day, if there's time for me to do some practicing, then I do that," and then she's quick to add, "most of the time, there's not."

So she finds ways to create time. She outsources the unimportant things. "The dishes need to get done," she states matter-of-factly. "But I don't have to do them. So a high school girl comes by a couple times a week and does dishes and sweeps the floor. I pay her to do the things that I don't have to do. I can't pay her to take my place reading stories to my kids. Then I can get everything done that I need to do in a day."

You don't have to pay someone to do those other chores. Maybe you just assign another family member or colleague to do some of those outsourceable things. Maybe you decline some opportunities that you would normally say "yes" to. And maybe, perish the thought, some of those things that fall farther down your list of passions, slide by undone from time to time.

Jenny, with her picture-perfect family, admits there are times when she notices her kids' noses haven't been wiped, or there are stains on their clothes at the grocery store, or even the unthinkable, they arrive at church with curlers in their hair and she has to make a quick stop in the restroom to correct the oversight. "People don't mind," she adds coyly. "They are forgiving."

And she is better off because of her passions. She is better at both mothering and music. The one helps the other and vice versa. She is more alive at both because she has found something that makes her soul sing.

Nothing great in the world has been accomplished without passion.

~ Georg Wilhelm Friedrich Hegel

It is still easier to say than to actually do. After a full day of work, or managing a household, or both, we get home and try to muster up whatever energy we can manage. And with that energy, we make Hamburger Helper, or oversee the distributive property of multiplication, or sort delicates from denims, or whack weeds, or surf channels, or browse websites, or read stories, or just try to keep our head above the seemingly rising water level. It's tough. No one is sugar-coating it and making it seem like any one of us is sitting around with disposable time waiting to direct it toward some yearning passion.

To help, we wanted to devote a whole month of TV segments to the topic of Finding Balance. Amanda Dickson is a popular speaker, author, and radio personality. She's got the kind of contagious enthusiasm you can feel just by her smiling at you.

We asked her to kick off the theme for the month and help us know what we have to do to "find balance."

Amanda had spent weeks with the internal debate of what has to happen to find balance. She came up with her outline of how to achieve that ever-elusive goal. She talked with experts. She read books. She looked deep inside herself. We collaborated with her to unveil her four step plan. We dispatched our art department to create some special full-screen graphics to post on the screen with her rules to find balance.

She had a guide for a balance check. She was going to help people realize that their "best is good enough," no matter what the outcome. She had ways to help viewers manage their expectations. As the date approached, she gathered her stories and anecdotes. She wrote up an article for us to post on our website. We wrote promotional commercials touting her appearance and peppered the airwaves. It had been on our radar for over a month and Amanda had been gearing up for the appearance for that same amount of time. Then the day finally arrived.

Minutes before the show, Amanda climbed into an elevator on her way to the studio. As she stepped in, she met her friend Emily Watts. Emily is a smart and sensible woman, full of wit and wisdom, and generous with her observations.

"Hello Amanda, I haven't seen you in a while. What are you up to?" the conversation must have gone.

"Oh Emily, it's great to see you. I'm on my way right now to the TV studio. I'm helping to kick off the theme for the month on Finding Balance. I've been working for weeks trying to figure out exactly what you need to find balance."

And with that, Emily cocked her head a bit and looked right at Amanda. Then her simple words turned profound. "Amanda. You don't need to find balance. You need to find priorities."

Amanda's heart sank a fraction of a millimeter. She knew it was true. We can try all we want to have everything evenly balanced. We can spend the exact same amount of time on work and family and community and PTA and church and volunteer service. We can try to balance fun with serious. We can try to balance work with play. We can try to balance jogging with eating double fudge brownie ripple ice cream and a big ol' piece of chocolate crème pie. That might get us evenly spread out. But it doesn't do much more than that. Being balanced makes us a slave to some giant imaginary weighing scale where we want both sides perfectly weighted. But it doesn't guarantee that we get the things done that matter the most to us.

Amanda let that bombshell distill in her mind on her way to the studio. And then, when the red lights went on and we turned to her to help us find balance, she tossed that same bombshell our direction. It did the same thing to our psyches that it did to hers. We still went through the motions of the rest of her segment. She still talked about her balance check and reminded us to manage our expectations. The artistically crafted graphics popped up on cue. Everything went off as planned.

But for the rest of the segment and for the rest of the segments that month we realized that we were pursuing something that wasn't really what it appeared to be on the outside. We don't want balance. We want priorities.

Balance will never get you chasing passions. Priorities will. At some point, you have to say to your heart and your head that you have to pursue your passion.

DARIN-ISM NO. 11

Pursuing passions doesn't take you away from being a good parent, spouse or friend. It actually makes you a better one.

Many of our TV viewers are women and for them, pursuing their passions can be a different ballgame than for men. Some of the same attributes that make them wonderful, caring, nurturing, and loving people, can also make it a little more challenging to grab the bull by the horns and aggressively go after their dreams. Enter Brett Harward. Brett is a business guru who has worked with thousands of businesses and individuals around the world, helping them get what they want out of life. Knowing that many of our viewers needed a little help in marketing their ambitions and dreams, we asked Brett to come on TV to share his expertise.

A few days ahead of the segment, I happened to see several strange heads walking back to the studio. The heads weren't necessarily strange. It was just that I didn't recognize them. I knew that Brett was going to be in town and some other contacts in the building had mentioned they might show him around. On a hunch, I jogged back to the studio to meet Brett and two other gentlemen from our TV marketing department.

I was excited to meet him and paint the picture of what we were looking for. "Many of our viewers," I began, "have some dream or passion, but they just don't know how to pursue it successfully. They might have some interest in photography and they want to turn it into a business. They might want to start a pre-school in their neighborhood and they need to get the word out. They might have an etsy site online but they don't know how to present their things."

They all seemed to be following my train of thought as I went along. In conclusion, I wrapped it up with my same examples. "So we want to help that aspiring photographer, or that pre-school teacher, or that woman with the etsy site. We want to give them the knowledge they need to succeed with their dreams."

There was an awkward pause. The three of them glanced nervously at each other and then back at me. Finally one of them spoke, "I think we know about photography, and pre-school. But I don't think we have a clue what an etsy site is."

It was then that I realized that I was talking to three men who likely never had nor never would have cause to go shopping online for handmade crafts or fashion accessories. Once I explained that etsy was simply an online central market for thousands of crafters, artisans and entrepreneurs to sell handmade wares, they understood exactly.

Brett had great ideas for the segment and shared how women often focus on the wrong wording or the wrong colors in their marketing. He pointed out how they need to market the benefits and not just the features. It was great information for anyone needing help in marketing their passion.

Brett is also the author of the book, "The 5 Laws That Determine All of Life's Outcomes." One of his laws is the law of vision. He explains how we need to alter our vision or the way we look at our daily life. If you can alter your vision, you can see how you can find time for your passions.

We all have 24 hours a day. There's no way that any of us get any more or any fewer than 24. And we each get the choice every day to decide how to trade those 24 hours for whatever we want. If you think there's some magic pill that will suddenly grant you an extra hour, then I hate to disappoint.

Most of us can view our day as a pie chart. You divide your day up into increments or slices of pie. For many people, work can be the biggest chunk of pie. Whether you go to a business and punch a card or stay home and run a household, it's a huge piece of pie. For those running a household, you could even slice that piece of pie in various smaller pieces such as cleaning, cooking, running errands, taking care of children and watching your favorite TV show (as long as I'm on it). Next, we all have to sleep. That's a slice of pie you can't do without. Don't forget spending quality time with the family, eating meals, exercise, personal time, social endeavors, and whatever other slices you are able to carve out of your 24-hour pie.

You can try to find extra time for your passions, but whatever you do, you have to take part of another slice for it. You can't just create new slices. And most of us have felt a little out of balance as one slice is starting to suffer when we keep carving away at it.

It's the proverbial "get up 15 minutes earlier" rule. You know that one. Do you want to read your favorite book, but you just can't find any time? Just "get up 15 minutes earlier" in the morning. Need some time for spiritual reflection? Just "get up 15 minutes earlier" in the morning. Need to exercise? Just "get up 15 minutes earlier" in the morning. Falling behind with some chores like cleaning out the fridge or dusting the bookshelves? Just "get up 15 minutes earlier" for each of those. You keep at it until you're getting up in the middle of the night.

And there's a price to pay. Mainly, you're exhausted! Next thing you know, you're dozing off in the middle of the day while you're supposed to be watching the kids, only to wake up and find peanut butter smeared all over the front of the fridge with the culprits taking aim at your clean laundry basket. Or at work, you happen to nod off at your computer only to have your boss catch you as your head snaps back leaving a puddle of drool on the desk and a red mark on your forehead where your head was resting on the keyboard. Not that I have done any of those things.

The point is that you can't create new hours. But what Brett taught me is something that is almost as good.

Instead of thinking of your day as a pie with 24 hours, think of it as a cake with 24 hours. Cakes are very different from pies simply because they have various heights whereas pies are just one layer.

As we go through life, we try to multi-task and get several things done at the same time. We do work from home. We try to resolve personal matters from work. We talk on the phone while driving. We text while eating family dinner. We browse the web while we try to have a conversation with our spouse. And we listen to how our children's school day went while we process that day's bills. It doesn't work. But picture devoting real concentrated time on some things and imagine how much more you could do.

The more intense time you want to spend on a slice of cake, the taller the cake might be. Sleep isn't that critical for concentration. That can simply be a one layer Pillsbury Confetti cake with frosting from the can. Don't waste time on that one. Maybe you want to have some spiritual reflection time in the morning. Make that a double layer carrot cake with homemade cream cheese frosting. It doesn't have to be a big slice since you're making it more intense. Instead of being distracted as you spend time with your kids, give them your undivided attention with a triple-decker chocolate fudge torte and throw on some sprinkles. Work could be a sour cream bundt coffee cake which is taller than average; focus on what you're doing while you're there and do it well, then move on and leave it behind. And of course, you might not have a lot of space left for your cake, so make sure you have a four-layer Italian Wedding cake slice for your spouse. Make it quality cake, er, I mean time.

Brett's pie chart, or cake chart, shows a whole new way to look at how we divvy up time. There's an extra element to it. There's depth to our time. It's more than just setting a timer for an activity. It's measuring how intently we are involved. If you can't spend a whole hour out stargazing, just spend 15 minutes with a quick search for a constellation and be done with your quick fix. If you're too busy to allot a whole round of golf, hit half a bucket of balls and be done with it. If you don't have time to read a chapter in your favorite book, just read a page or two, get your fix, put it down and get back with the rest of your hectic schedule.

Generally, perfectionists set themselves up for failure. They figure if they can't do it right, if they can't give the amount of time they deem appropriate, then it's not worth doing. They postpone their engagement with their passion. They procrastinate doing whatever they love assuming the perfect time will roll around sooner or later. It's always later. And procrastination is the mother of depression. Many times when we are depressed, it's because something has been procrastinated. Lose the train of thought that you need to have the whole enchilada of time that you would normally want. Be happy if you just get a bite of that enchilada. Have your taste of your passion. Do it intently. Savor the flavor. Reap the benefit from engaging in your passion, no matter how short a time it was.

Brett related the story of a young man he worked with. He was working at a local auto parts store and anxious to figure out how to make more of his career. He wanted a better position and more money. In order to help him take advantage of the cake chart, or the concept of depth and intensity, Brett taught him a simple phrase, "I'm all over it."

This was the kind of establishment where jobs were always pushed from person to person, no one wanting to pick up the ball and take care of business. Now this young man was not only being asked to do those jobs, but was asked to emphatically cry out, "I'm all over it!" New shipment arrives and needs to be stocked on the shelves? "I'm all over it!" Customer walks in the front door needing help? "I'm all over it!" Clean up on aisle 4? "I'm all over it!"

At first, the upper management laughed at his enthusiasm. But after the chuckling died down, they noticed the intensity with which he served customers and did his job. The customers noticed it, too. They loved his dedication and energy. They specifically asked for him to help them. His pay got bumped up a couple bucks an hour after a few weeks. Soon after that, he got another raise. He was promoted first to assistant manager, and then to commercial manager, and more money followed. Within a year from the time he first uttered, "I'm all over it ," he was making more money than the other employees who had been there much longer, including the manager.

He had taken the same piece of cake that everyone else had, but had built it into a monstrous multi-level cake with custard, and fruit fillings between the layers, and mounds of butter cream frosting on top.

Don't believe yourself when you try to rationalize that you don't have time. You have time, even just a fractional sliver that you can use with all the intensity that your passion deserves. Don't wait for some magical balance to be achieved in your life's schedule. Waiting won't make it happen. Adjust your priorities to make sure that there's a little slice just for you and your passions.

12

Six Envelopes, Six Checks, Mission Accomplished

Finding financing for your Passion

When it comes to holidays, Easter has to be pretty good. Think about it.

There generally aren't any familial pressures. It's not like in-laws are protesting, "But you spent Easter with that side of the family last year."

The food is pretty much no-fail. As long as you have plenty of Cadbury eggs, you don't skimp on the Reese's eggs, and you realize that most people really don't like Peeps, you can't go wrong.

And there aren't any high expectations of presents. There generally aren't tears on Sunday morning because the Easter Bunny didn't drop off a bike or an Xboxox gaming console.

In our family, you might get a small gift or two, and call it good. That, and your basket full of Starburst jelly beans and pastel M&Ms make for a nice haul.

One year, the "gifting" budget was a little leaner than in past years. So my wife and I explained that we wouldn't get each other gifts. We were both fine with that. Then I remembered that someone had given me a large bulk roll of wrapping paper. Now, in my mind, wrapping paper isn't a gift. Wrapping paper is what goes around the gift. (And how do you wrap wrapping paper? It's already wrapped. If you wrap it, how does the person know when to stop unwrapping? They keep ripping through the layers of the roll not realizing that the paper actually is the gift.) But my wife gets into anything that has to do with parties and decorating. So wrapping paper was her well-received Easter gift.

Over the next days, the roll of pink and green polka-dotted paper was a constant reminder to her that she hadn't given me a gift. She felt the scales of gift giving had been thrown out of balance. In my mind there wasn't an imbalance. Remember, it was a free roll of wrapping paper. But in her mind, it was a disturbance in the hospitality force.

So on Spring Break, our family took a little trip to a nearby retail center. There were fun stores full of gadgets and gizmos, perfect for window shopping. We strolled into an Apple store. While we played with all the electronic toys and accessories with cool colors, my wife disappeared for a second. When she returned to interrupt our software test-driving, she confessed that she had bought me an adapter for my iPod.

"You what?" my neck jerked my head sideways toward her.

"I bought you an adapter for your iPod," she beamed as she opened her purse to show me the plunder of her pursuit.

"Why did you do that?"

"Because you need one."

"I don't need one."

"Yes, you do," she went on. "That way, you don't have to charge it on my docking station. You can charge in on your own whenever you want."

"No," I pleaded. "I really don't need one. I can charge it on the computer if I need to do that. And I only charge it about once a week anyway. And for that, I can even charge it overnight on your docking station."

"No," she countered. "You need one. It's your Easter present. You got me one, and I'm getting you one."

"No, seriously," I went on, now completely forgetting whatever gadget I had been playing with before the iPod charger interruption had begun. "I don't need it. It's not a 'need.' It's not even a 'want.' How much did it cost? Even if it's only 10 dollars, it would be ten dollars that I would much rather spend on something that I really enjoy. I would rather spend that ten dollars and take the family bowling. I would rather go and get French fries for everyone. There are things that I enjoy doing, and I would rather spend the money on that."

After my plea, my wife confessed that the adapter was actually 30 dollars. That was the clincher. After she considered the matter, she agreed that it was not something I needed, so with her permission, I decided to return the purchase. With our limited funds, I didn't want to spend resources on something that wasn't my passion in place of something that was my passion.

Do what you love and do it often.
- *The Holstee Manifesto*

We all have financial resources at our disposal. And we all get to decide how we want to spend those resources. Now pursuing passions can get expensive. If going for a walk around the block is your passion, or watching birds in your back yard, or collecting those plastic bags that newspapers come in on rainy days, then bully for you. You are lucky enough to have a passion that is pretty much going to cost you next-to-nothing. Check that. It's going to cost you nothing. But if your passion is gourmet cooking or driving fancy race cars or traveling to tiny countries that are surrounded by water and can only be reached by charter planes, then you're going to have to balance your passion with your purse strings. (You might have to try to find a purse with strings first. Does anyone make those?)

If you were hoping there would be some unknown pearls of wisdom concealed in these pages telling you how to suddenly grow rich, you might be sorely disappointed. I don't know what the lottery numbers are going to be next week. I don't know of any way to rig the Publisher's Clearinghouse Sweepstakes. And I don't think there's a secret to win that contest on the back of the cereal box you were reading this morning. If you can figure those things out on your own, please send me an email and we'll buy a private island somewhere.

The key is to take a different view of the finances that you already have. It takes a little bit of soul-searching to look at exactly where you're spending your money and what you're getting in return. Then you have to ask if it's worth it.

I am not interested in money.
I just want to be wonderful.
- Marilyn Monroe

I had been working in Pocatello, Idaho for several years, when a change in management prompted me to seek a change in employment. The short story: the new manager and I didn't share the same passions.

I stumbled across a job opening at a small, neglected station in Peoria. It wasn't a job I was interested in. The short story: I applied anyway.

It was fueled by the opportunity to exercise my passions and do what I enjoyed. It was definitely NOT fueled by more pay.

The General Manager, Bill Lamb, had a little sit-down heart-to-heart with me. He had just shown me around the run-down facilities and then came the "money talk." He was not even able to match the humble wages I was already making.

"But it's not just about money," he started. That was easy for him to say. He was driving a nice, luxury, company car, and I can guarantee that he was making a whole lot more than what he was offering me. I started to dig in my heels.

"You have to think of finances as an investment. When you think about it, everything we spend money on is an investment. If you go out and buy a boat, you are trading that money for something. You are investing it in the hopes that you will be happier. When you spend money to go back to school, you are investing in your education. When you buy a new suit, you are investing in your image. Much of what we spend money on is simply an investment in ourselves."

Then he explained how that applied to me. "Even though you would have to take a cut in salary to come here, you have to think of that as an investment in yourself. It's just like you are paying the difference in money to help you stretch your creative muscles. You're learning new skills that will make you a better employee, weatherman, and person. You are investing in yourself."

It was a cheap, manipulative, psychological ploy. It was just a way to get me to come work for him even though it didn't make financial sense. But I bought it.

DARIN-ISM NO. 12

Pursuing passions should be considered an investment in yourself.

And the investment paid off. While I started out by going backwards financially, I got ahead of the game professionally with a few years of investing in myself and broadening the skills that go along with my passion for creativity. For five years, I worked with Bill and other creative personnel in Peoria until I was given the opportunity to extend my creativity even more. I made a jump I would never have dreamed of. I lept more than

100 markets to take a job as a "creative weatherman" in the sixth largest market, Boston.

Dr. Liz is one of those unique people who makes you feel better after just a brief encounter. She always has a warm smile and an equally warm greeting. Her real name is Liz Hale, but since she's a therapist, we affectionately just call her Dr. Liz. Before our TV show ever debuted, Dr. Liz was on board as a regular. She had wonderful and empathetic counsel for families and couples and anyone struggling to have better relationships. Dr. Liz was our monthly therapy session.

But Dr. Liz had her own therapy, and she found a way to get it for free.

When she moved from Seattle to Salt Lake City to be a program manager for a therapy and counseling office, it was just at the time her new employer was getting ready to move locations. They had eyed the majestic Pioneer Theatre for their office space and got ready to make the switch. The problem was that the old Pioneer Theatre looked like, well, it looked like an old theatre. It didn't feel like a warm and inviting place where people could let their guard down and open up.

"For some crazy reason," Dr. Liz admits, "they asked me to help pick out colors and furnishings and décor. It was likely desperation."

But Dr. Liz was just the person for the job. She had always been interested in the psychology of color and how design and the aesthetics of a room can create a sense of calm and well-being. There was one problem. Dr. Liz was not an interior designer. She didn't have any training. She hadn't taken any classes. It would be as if I offered to remove your tonsils. I might be interested, but I still don't have a clue about it. And chances are, you wouldn't be saying "ahhhh" to me anytime in the near future.

Design and décor became her passion. It wasn't an official work assignment, so she couldn't just take the afternoon off and go browsing for accessories. That didn't bother her. She loved doing it whenever and wherever she could.

It kept coming back to her lack of training. She didn't have a budget to go take a class. She had to somehow figure out how to do what she loved to do, and it had to be free.

Dr. Liz headed down to the local RC Willey furniture store and tracked down a designer. It was there that she met Debra Tucker. It was a refreshing spring evening as she walked briskly into the store. She spotted Debra wearing a smart suit and a warm smile. From that first meeting, she sensed it was the start of something special.

"I told her I wanted to learn everything about design. I told her about my project and I asked her to help me. I asked her to be my mentor. I shadowed her. I followed her around and tried to learn everything I could by watching her. I'd come down whenever I could and sometimes would stay until the store closed at 10:00 at night. She was generous with me. She taught me all those things I needed so much to know and what I truly wanted to do."

And so, late into the night, Liz would look over Debra's shoulder. She would ask why that carpet color went with that armoire. She would ask what made that big framed painting the right scale. She would ask how those two printed fabrics complemented each other. In Debra, she had her own private tutor. And Dr. Liz learned to be a skilled and artistic decorator without ever taking so much as a class. All because she asked a talented, kind, and willing person to help teach her.

Armed with the tools, Dr. Liz started living her passion. "I was in heaven as I shopped and shopped for the right items. I wanted to create a space that conveyed respect for visitors and interest in them. I still remember when I spotted the perfect couch," she remembers wistfully. It was part-leather and part-rich Ralph Lauren-esque fabric. "It was just special. It just said 'we care about you' to clients who would come in."

Then she spotted a purple rug. Who would have ever dreamed a purple rug would go with that couch? But Liz remembered a seed that another designing mentor had planted in her head and she put the two together. It was a perfect match. "It was gorgeous!" she almost whispered, remembering the pairing. She continued on, piece by piece until she had created a masterpiece of a space, which was warm and welcoming.

With one smashing success under her belt, she traveled to her father's home in Star Valley, Wyoming. Since the fireplace was out of code, she had it torn out. One thing led to another and she turned her fashion focus on the rest of the house.

"I wasn't afraid of mistakes at that point. I knew that if I made a mistake, it wasn't the end of the world. I created this mono-chromatic space for him. There was a new fireplace, new carpet, new granite, and in the end it was this beautiful "western elegance" themed home."

Anxious for another blank canvas, she started in her own townhouse. "Initially, I wouldn't have been too brave, but I had learned from some wonderful people. I painted the walls a rich, dark color. It's Char Brown which is perfect. I have this giant zebra painting where all you can see is stripes and a big eye. And I love chaise lounges so much that I got two of them. That's all I have in my living room, just these two oversized, black chaise lounges. Even Debra questioned me on it. 'Are you sure you want two of them?' she asked. I had to reassure her that it was exactly what I wanted."

Debra should have known. She was the one who taught her. She was the one who set the decorating passion on fire. Now she just had to get out of the way. Dr. Liz discovered that decorating was her own therapy, and she had found a solution to get the skills for this therapy session for free.

Dr. Liz isn't a self-taught decorator. She learned from the best. She just didn't have to pay a dime for all the fuel for her passion. And it was all because she asked for it. "I'm never hesitant to ask for things. I have discovered that there are people out there who are willing to be our mentors if we let them. I did that with Debra and now we are the dearest of friends, still to this day."

You could tell just by looking at Liz that she loves being creative. She has a dramatic flair in her wardrobe as well as her home décor. On TV, she invariably wears a one-of-a-kind necklace that might be huge, chunky stones. Maybe it's some hand swirled silver. It could be some eye-catching crystals. It should come as no surprise what happened recently when she showed up for a TV segment with an impressive and beautiful big necklace.

"Liz, that is a beautiful necklace. Where did you get that?" Brooke asked her.

"Well, funny you should ask," Dr. Liz started in. "I was up at one of my favorite boutiques, Poletti's up on Highland, and they have this woman there who makes these necklaces. They are just these beautiful works of art. So I went up to her and said, 'I would love to learn how to do that. Can I be your assistant? Can I help you in any way? I will work for free just to be trained and to learn how you do that.'"

It might seem like an odd scene. Picture a professional, highly trained therapist sitting in a small boutique helping a jewelry artisan put together a necklace. But Dr. Liz is just getting more free fuel for her passion.

There are some people who live in a dream world, and there are some who face reality. And then there are those who turn one into the other.
- Douglas H. Everett

It's easy to commit to some goal of pursuing a passion. There's no real investment though, so it's easy to back out when it gets tough. How hard is it to say you'll do something? Not very. How hard is it to actually do it when you hit the brick wall? Very. So one trick is to make a commitment when you're feeling strong, that guarantees you have an incentive even when you're weak.

Lisa J. Peck is known as the "Step It Up Queen." She motivates people to take things to the next level. She is great at motivating and moving others. When it came to herself, she sometimes had a hard time committing the resources, including financial, to do what needed to get done.

So she convened an unconventional group. She gathered five other friends for a mastermind team that would hold each other accountable for their goals.

Doug Nielsen wanted to finish up writing a picture book. Jason Alba wanted to create a series of videos. Brad Barton wanted to improve his marketing process. Mitch Seehusen wanted to revamp his website and look at marketing. Julie Morrison wanted to make a packet for entrepreneurs. And Lisa wanted to overhaul her website and give it a new look. She wanted to add some MP3s, toss in some new text, and include some interview clips with her motivational advice.

Most of those goals were going to involve some financial commitment. But everyone in the group had experienced a hard time buckling down and just doing what they needed to do.

This time was going to be different. Everyone brought $150 to the table. It was all tossed into the pot and they all had 90 days to accomplish their individual goals, or else. The goals were the same, but this time, there was an investment. If you didn't accomplish your goal, you ran the risk of losing some or all your money.

Over the next 90 days, all six of the mastermind teammates held each other responsible for what they had pledged to do. "There's always a creative solution to get what you need," Lisa points out. "If you look for it, there's a way. Is there a trade you can make? Are there people out there who can help out with the thing that you need?"

In Lisa's case, she used Jason's help. "He was a great interviewer and he was able to interview me for some of the website content. He was articulate and great at it. Some of the things I had postponed doing, I was able to do for free because of him."

And when it came time to hire out some of the things that needed a paid professional, Lisa had no problem forking over the cash to get the job done. If she didn't, she was going to lose her $150, not to mention her pride.

"If you really want something, then why are you putting it off? Why are you finding other things that are more important?"

And Lisa certainly has other things to spend money on that could seem more important. She has 12 kids, seven still living at home, ages 19 down to 2, with five of them teenagers. Do you have any idea how expensive teenagers can be? They can run up a tab to rival the national debt just on makeup, trips to the mall, and Justin Bieber downloads on iTunes.

"But if you really want something," she points out, "if you want it enough, it's going to work. You're going to find a solution. And it's important to find the solution and do what you love to do. I just read something that says people who work really hard at what they love, live longer. Those who are actively involved and passionate about something they love are less stressed. If you're really stepping it up, you're going to find a creative solution."

It is in all of us to defy expectations, to go into the world and to be brave, and to want, to need, to hunger for adventures, to embrace change and chance, so that we may breathe and know what it is to be free.

~ Mae Cherrette

Money can be powerful. It can keep us from doing the things we really want to do. So the opposite should be true. It can help motivate us to do the things we really want to do. That's the theory of Ray Levtire who is good friends with money. He's a money guy who lets us pick his brain on TV.

He used money as his motivator a few years back. He is passionate about working with money, and working with people who need a little help with managing their money. He had been advising people for years, but one day decided he wanted to earn the title of Certified Financial Planner. That's the ultimate designation for people in that field. But it's basically like earning an advanced college degree.

It would mean that Ray would have to do the equivalent of two years of college courses and then pass a rigorous exam. The problem is that it's all done on your own. There is no deadline hanging over your head. There is no professor breathing down your neck. There is no lab instructor willing to give you extra help in exchange for candy bars from the college bookstore (not that I ever did that). This was just Ray on his own.

Finally after four long years, he had finished the course work. Up next, the mammoth two-day Certified Financial Planner test loomed. To make sure that the candidate was prepared, there were six practice tests. All Ray had to do was take the six practice tests, then ace the big one. But for some reason, he had a hard time knuckling down and taking the tests.

There was always something more interesting to do. Watching TV. Playing sports. Flossing teeth. It seemed that anything was more interesting than taking those practice tests. Ray still had the passion to earn the CFP accreditation. He just was having a hard time staying on task. So he employed the power of his old friends, the greenbacks.

He pulled out a checkbook and wrote out six checks for a hundred bucks each. Then he made each of them payable to an organization he loathed. There is nothing he would hate more than actually donating money to the group. He put the checks in individual envelopes, ready to mail out. Next he tracked down a colleague who just happened to work in the same office complex, someone he didn't even know very well.

He handed him the stack of money-stuffed envelopes with the instructions, "I want you to check with me every week. If I have taken the practice exam that week, then give me back the envelope for that week. If I haven't taken the test, mail it off."

Ray knew what would happen. "This guy didn't know me well enough to feel sorry for me if I hadn't taken the test. He just knew his job was to drop that envelope in the mail if I hadn't done what I was supposed to do."

One envelope made it to the postman. That was all it took. For Ray, who loved and understood the power of money, it was the perfect motivation. "Somehow I created the time that I needed. That money was all I needed to move things around and make things happen."

Five weeks later, he had recovered his five remaining sealed envelopes and was ready for the big test, which he aced on the first try.

He pulled out the old money motivation years later when he wanted to coach the JV lacrosse team at a local high school. Sports had been his passion in high school and college, and now that his daughter was picking up lacrosse, he felt passionate about it again. But coaching would mean he would have to leave work at 3:30 to get to practice. Since he was in the habit of cruising into work around 10:00 each morning, it hardly added up to a full day's work. So he figured he would try to get to work a little early. Just like the practice exam, the desire alone didn't quite hack it.

"So I told all the girls on the team that I needed to get to work by 6:45. I promised them all that I would text them when I got to work every morning. If I wasn't on time, I told them I would pay them each a dollar. That would end up being about 30 bucks every time. So I wasn't about to start shelling out that kind of money every morning," Ray confessed.

He coughed up the money once, and that was enough.

"People say they want to do something. They want to write a book, or take on a new hobby or something. But that's just it. It's just something they want to do. The trick is to make sure you actually follow through. There has to be some accountability, and if there's not, then it's just an idea."

Jeffrey R. Holland was the president of BYU while I was a student. He was a man full of passion. I still remember an address to the student body where he encouraged us to be civil and treat other teams with respect at sporting events. I can still remember him exhorting us to "kill them with kindness." And to this day, I think of his impassioned plea every time I'm tempted to boo "the other team."

He later issued an equally passionate plea to anyone who is tempted to let anything stand in the way of their passions:

"Opposition turns up almost anyplace something good has happened. There are cautions and considerations to make, but once there has been genuine illumination, beware the temptation to retreat from a good thing. If it was right when you... trusted it and lived for it, it is right now. Don't give up when the pressure mounts... Face your doubts. Master your fears. 'Cast not away therefore your confidence.' Stay the course and see the beauty of life unfold for you."

13

Leaving Your Trials On the Mountain

Passions trump ALL

When Kerstin Daynes married her husband Joel, she figured she was just starting on the journey she had always dreamed of. She dreamed of starting a family and raising a whole passel of little kids. Her promising, wonderful future was right at her fingertips. It was brimming with anticipation and hope and possibilities.

Year one, no kids had arrived. Year two, still nothing. Year three, Kerstin started to get a little concerned. Year four, Kerstin and Joel realized that their future was not aware of what they had planned out on their own. Someone hadn't clued the "future" in on what Kerstin and Joel had in mind.

Years earlier, Kerstin's appendix had burst. In the back of her mind, she knew that there was a slight chance that it might affect her ability to have children, but it was a slim chance and she had never given the thought much room in her mind. It had been crowded out by hopes and dreams of her growing family.

Now something else was taking over her thoughts. She was infertile.

"It's devastating," Kerstin admitted. "It redefines your life and who you are when life doesn't turn out the way you planned." Kerstin and her husband had invested lots of time, lots of emotion, and "we had just failed. We were devastated that nothing had worked."

Suddenly, the feelings were different. Now it was sorrow. Stress. Anger.

Kerstin would sit there enveloped in her feelings. They wrapped around her and became her life. It was all she could focus on. They tightened their grip until they prevented her from moving on in life.

"When you have those thoughts, they can be debilitating," she remembered. "You just sit there and those thoughts have this destructive ability to stop you dead in your tracks. They stop you from accomplishing things. They prevent you from being happy."

She needed a way to release it all, the pent up feelings of self-loathing and frustration and lack of fulfillment. She decided to chase them away. Literally.

She found a large park near her house where she could run. There was an expansive trail that wound around the foothills. And there she would go every day. She would lace up her shoes and just run. She would run at all times of the day. Mornings, she went running. Evenings, she went running. When things got overwhelming, she went running. A mile or two, three or four, five or six a day.

And there on the flatiron mesa overlooking the broad valley, she fired up a new passion. There, with an expansive vision that stretched for miles, she found that she could think differently. There, as she sailed through sawgrass and sycamores, she found she could control one small aspect of her life when so many other things were out of control.

Some people run to relieve stress. It was much more than that for Kerstin. It wasn't about getting rid of something. It was about gaining something. "It's something I can have control over and be successful. I can control when I drink Gatorade and when I hydrate. I know it's silly. But mentally, it's so empowering to me."

It was not only a way to keep her body healthy, but her mind as well.

But passions don't always supplant desires. Kerstin and Joel still yearned for a child.

After five years of trying on their own, they consulted with modern medicine, anxious to try anything that might offer a glimmer of success. Kerstin was poked and prodded more times than she can remember. They went through every possible way that might be an option. Because the root of the problem was hormonal, avenues that might be possible for others were closed to them.

They tried artificial insemination. They tried it again. And again and again.

In vitro fertilization was a possibility. Kerstin started up on the medication, but the procedure was cancelled when it was discovered her body wasn't responding. Doctors doubled up the dosage, but Kerstin said the result was "doubly worse." None of the embryos lived.

They were done.

And every time, Kerstin returned to the passion she knew all too well. She ran. She gained control over the hand that life had dealt her, at least in one small part.

"Passions are a way we can change directions in our lives," Kerstin told me on TV. We wanted her to inspire viewers with another passion she had discovered.

In the middle of her journey, Kerstin had discovered her love for writing. It started as a way to express her feelings. She found passion in being able to verbalize things that she would never tell people otherwise.

Joel encouraged her to share herself with others. He could see she was struggling with the raw feelings of her emotions and could see the healing benefit that came when she shared those thoughts with others through her literary passion. Writing blossomed. She launched into work on her book, '"Infertility: Help, Hope and Healing." She began blogging. She started forum groups. She had found a creative method to use her time to think of herself in a positive way, not a negative way.

"When we find these passions, like the one I found in my life, we find a glimpse of greatness. It's a part of something we can be great at. It's a way to use our talents in a way we didn't think of; to be positive in other people's lives."

Her writing was real. It shared raw emotions. It was very real to her, and writing about it provided healing that was also real. Between the writing and the running, Kerstin was able to channel her energy into things that she loved, things she was good at.

Kerstin and Joel made peace with themselves. They were who they were going to be. They accepted it.

And then something strange happened. It was after Kerstin had abandoned artificial insemination. It was after she had given up on in vitro fertilization. It was after she had come to grips with infertility.

It was in the midst of finding her passions. It was sometime after the running paths. It was tucked in between the blog and the book.

Kerstin got pregnant.

Kerstin calls little William an absolute miracle.

Even though William is now in school, Kerstin still clings to her passions. Their little boy was a dream come true, but Kerstin knows what any parent knows. Children aren't always the picture-perfect image in all those "Baby Gap" ads. "It's an absolute joy and very challenging in all different ways," Kerstin says of her life now.

Her book's message still pertains to her today. It's about finding passion. It's about using those passions to help you power through whatever obstacles are in your path. It doesn't matter if you're hoping for a child in the face of infertility, or encountering some other challenge.

"Passions have to continue to live in life. I continue to find these little passions. They are like little glimpses of greatness. It's easy to let other things in life overshadow them. But you have to find them and let them breathe.

"It's a little spark in life. It gives you greater meaning. Direction. Happiness. Light."

God created us to live with a single
passion, to joyfully display His supreme
excellence in all the spheres of Life. The
wasted life is the life without this passion.

~ *John Piper*

Rachel and Aaron Coleman were ecstatic when their daughter
Leah was born. She was fabulous and adorable. She was a
perfectly behaved baby who was quiet and content. The young
couple cooed and coddled their beautiful girl. It was just what
Rachel had dreamed it would be having a baby girl of her own.

The one-year checkup arrived for Rachel with Leah in tow.
The doctor ran through the litany of routine questions. "How's
her vision?"

"She's great," Rachel chipped in. "She can see anything."

The questions continued until the "How are her words?"

Rachel later confessed, "I was kind of embarrassed. I felt like
I was failing as a parent. I had to confess that she didn't say
anything. No Baba. No Dada. No Mama. She would sometimes
just mouth the word "hi" to other people if they would say "hi"
to her in the store. I would sit in the car and would say "hi" to
her and she would smile, mouth it back to me and raise her
eyebrows. But sounds never came out."

The doctor wasn't overly concerned about the confession. "If
she's not talking by 15 months, we'll look into it," he comforted
her.

At the time, Rachel had been in a band. A band practice had
run late and Rachel headed to her mother's house to pick up
Leah. When Rachel walked in, her mother stopped her before
Leah could see her. "Just call her," she whispered. "Call her
name."

Cautiously, Rachel called out, "Leah." There was no reaction.
A second "Leah" got the same non-response.

It caught in her throat. That was it. She knew that at a year, her own daughter should recognize a mother's voice. It felt like a slap in the face as it dawned on her, that her beautiful baby girl had never been able to hear a thing. The whisperings, the lullabies, the cuddling and coddling. Leah had never heard a sound.

Rachel and Aaron mourned for their daughter. They cried. But as they did, they noticed that Leah was watching them with a puzzled and confused look. For Leah, nothing had changed on that December evening when her mother had called her name. Leah was deaf, but she had always been deaf. It was only Rachel and Aaron who had discovered what had been there all along.

It dawned on Rachel that it was up to her to find something new. She had to discover a way to communicate with Leah. She had to learn some way to explore Leah's world with her.

It was a wake-up call that automatically changed Rachel's passions. "Up until that point, my passion was my music. I was in a band and that was my life. I grew up singing. It was just what we did. And suddenly, it seemed like such a waste of time. I immediately put that passion down and picked up a new one. Suddenly, all I could think about was finding a way to communicate with her. We needed to find something new, and that became my passion."

Rachel immersed herself in learning all she could. While other parents with non-verbal children would focus on wanting the child to speak, Rachel took a different approach. She simply wanted to be able to communicate with her. She didn't worry about speaking. She zeroed in on sign language.

Because of a mother's drive and zeal and passion, it took Leah less than a year and she was out-communicating her speaking peers. She could communicate, or speak in her own way. She could "say" that she was tired. She could "say" that she wanted to play outside. She could "say" that she wanted goldfish crackers.

And then Rachel's passion hit a roadblock. "I discovered the standard. We asked a woman from a state agency assigned to our case what we could expect. She basically said that when Leah graduates from high school, she will be at a 3rd grade reading level. I couldn't believe that anyone found that acceptable. I turned to her and bluntly asked, 'What are you doing wrong?'"

"That was what fueled my passion. I realized I wasn't willing to accept that standard. We couldn't just put her in a school and hope. It scared me to death. Here was a child whose only information is expressly communicated to her. She had no access to TV or radio or even overhearing something. Everything she would know would be because someone sat down and expressly told her."

Rachel and Aaron continued to teach Leah sign language. She picked it up rapidly. Life had finally slowed enough to let the trio catch their breath. It was then that the young family thought about adding another child. "We even thought it would be cool to have another deaf child. Wouldn't that be great? We're both pretty good at signing. We could handle that."

As the second pregnancy progressed, a routine ultrasound was scheduled. Rachel and Aaron were about to be knocked off their feet a second time.

Their child had hydrocephalus. It was inhibiting the growth of the brain. There were other complications, maybe even spina bifida. "Just as we were on our feet again, just as we had caught our breath, just as we were ready to move forward, this was a blow we just weren't prepared for. We went home and cried...again," she remembered.

Lucy was born early, and for 9 months, she had one mode. Fists clenched, head thrown back, and screaming. Rachel's nerves were fried. She was tired. She was frustrated.

And then her passions kicked in. She realized that she would just have to learn some new things

But even with her passion for signing, she was meeting with frustration. There were fewer and fewer family members who could keep up with it. Older sister Leah was being left out more and more. Dear friends had stopped inviting her over. Family invitations to see a movie weren't extended. Even adults would overlook her or intentionally leave her out, simply because they couldn't communicate with her. For Rachel, it felt like another slap in the face.

The ah-ha moment came for Rachel one warm afternoon at soccer practice. Leah was out running across the field, kicking the ball through the blades of green when the coach approached another young boy and asked him to be Leah's partner for a drill. "I don't want to be her partner," Rachel overheard the boy plead. "She can't even talk. She can't understand me. I don't want to play with her."

That was it. Rachel realized that she had to do something to make a difference for her daughter.

"I went straight to her pre-school. I told them I knew sign language. I wanted to do a story time. It was simple stuff. Brown Bear, Brown Bear stuff. Simple. I told them I was going to do story time twice a week. They were thrilled. And so was I."

The next week at soccer practice, Leah was out again chasing around the field when the boy arrived. He spotted her and made a beeline to her. His index fingers interlocked back and forth. "Friend," he said. He wiggled his hands with a 'hang loose' gesture. "Play." And then he clapped his hands together with just his outstretched fingers. "Ball."

He didn't take a course. He simply remembered three words. Yet Rachel saw how it changed how he could communicate with her child. She went home that day and began scheming with her sister, Emily.

Rachel and Emily had been "best siblings" for years. They had plotted and planned together their whole lives. And now, Rachel needed Emily to help her put together a plan to teach others to sign. They had to find a way to open up the world for Leah and others. They had to discover how to spread the passion.

They knew they had to make a video. It was going to be about singing, and full of music and rhythm and movement. Even though Rachel had sworn off music from the night of the late band practice where she discovered Leah's hearing loss, there was now enough drive and energy to help her recant it.

When plans began to get serious for the video, Leah was 4 and Lucy was 2. Emily told her sister Rachel to write a song for the video. "I'm not really a singer. Emily knew that, but she just told me to come up with something. I took Lucy in another room for an amazing 20 minutes. When I came back, I had two songs. The first one was the theme song and the second was "Show Me a Sign."

"It was basically a heartfelt plea for Lucy to show us something. I wanted to see some evidence that she was in there and could do something. The doctors had told us that Lucy was just retarded and would never sign. She was just like a doll. A big stiff two-year-old doll. I would just carry her everywhere I went. So I put that big two-year-old doll down and sang to her 'Show Me a Sign'.

As she finished, she looked at Lucy. That big stiff two-year-old doll picked up one fist and slowly but deliberately tapped it against her other fist, the sign for "more."

"Do you want more?" her mother asked.

Lucy's eyes got big and Rachel realized her daughter was signing. In her own way, she was talking.

The video production of Signing Times had changed countless lives by the time I met Rachel and interviewed her on TV. The first video had paved the way for many more to come. It had taken her a year to make that first video. At the time, she guessed she would make 100 copies and it would simply help people communicate with her daughter. She had no idea what would come from it.

You could see the impact that Signing Times had on her and her family. An even greater impact stretches far beyond those family borders. There are now 32 Signing Times CDs. Rachel has been on *The Today Show* and in *Ladies Home Journal*. She's been nominated for an Emmy. Signing Times has been on public TV, *Nick Jr.* and has won a slew of awards. Rachel travels the world educating and encouraging parents who have had their lives changed by Signing Times. It's a life she never dreamed of nor anticipated.

It started simply as a passion to help her daughter.

Today, Leah is a young teenager who is fluent in English and ASL. She has been mainstreamed into school where she has an interpreter. She chose to receive a cochlear implant when she was seven to improve her speech and listening skills.

"She is a great kid who is not vanilla in any way. She has personality and attitude and speaks very properly," Rachel is proud to announce. "Her deafness has been a fabulous filter for her. She doesn't know any bad words and didn't even know what to say about kids when she wanted to say something bad. She doesn't have any sarcasm or sassiness. She has a wonderful sweetness and maturity about her."

"And Lucy can talk, type and text now. We help her with some feeding and grooming but there are many things she can do on her own. She is brilliant and can hear a song once and sing it to you. She plays in a special soccer league and can swim. She'll tell you she's going to go run around...in her auto cart. And she can push her manual chair. She developed fine motor skills when no one believed she could do anything. She has been mainstreamed since Kindergarten and is great in school. Signing Times helped Lucy find her voice."

Rachel hears stories that continue to feed her passion. When she speaks or performs, parents line up for hours to share their experiences with her. Sometimes with tears in their eyes, and always with emotion in their hearts, they thank her for what she has done for them.

It started out as a challenge. An overwhelming, seemingly devastating, challenge. But passion kicked in to overcome that challenge. And when it did, lives changed.

"It's not just giving people hope. It's giving them access to possibilities. It's giving them the chance to have an amazing life."

I have already introduced you to Sheryl McGlochlin. She's the outdoor enthusiast who has never met a hike she didn't like. Her passion for hiking and all things outdoorsy is infectious and something we admire every time she does a segment on TV. Her passion is obvious. How she stumbled across it is something few people know.

Her story starts in 1993 when her son was just 9 years old. He had a friend Sheryl says we can just call "Steve." Now, how a 9-

year-old boy can cause such a downward spiral is beyond me, but Sheryl attests that her son's friend was quick-witted, smart, athletic and manipulative. He would do or say things that would push her buttons and delight in the reaction it provided. "Now I think, as I look back on this, that he was highly entertained by how easily he could get under my skin and drive me crazy. Just imagine being 'pecked at' nearly every day for 10 years. Any ONE 'pecking' wasn't a big deal, but when you combine this little torture on a daily, weekly, monthly and yearly amount, it adds up."

DARIN-ISM NO. 13

Don't allow the darkness of despair to steal your glimmers of greatness.

Sheryl allowed herself to be pecked into a dark and lonely place. Over the course of a decade, it got worse and worse. She was angry with her husband for not fixing the problem. Images of Steve dominated her thoughts and haunted her life. When there were family parties, she simply wanted to talk about Steve and how miserable he made her life. Not surprisingly, no one wanted to listen. Her anger, at times, turned to rage as the toxic feelings continued to build up.

She frighteningly confesses, "At one point, I hated him so much that I know if I had a gun, I would have shot him." Instead, she seriously considered just running away. She pictured just packing up and leaving it all behind. But her responsibilities as a mother kept her from doing that. And instead, she felt even more trapped by her dark and miserable situation and her tormentor, Steve.

"I thought, 'If I can't run away from home, then I'll go to my favorite restaurant, *The Mikado*, and I'll eat until I am happy again.' Fortunately for me, they were closed since it was between the lunch and dinner hours. What else could I do to relieve my agony? I sat in my car and cried. I felt helpless. I didn't know where I could turn for help. I cried some more."

Then, with no other recourse, she started to pray. In complete despair and through tear-choked hopelessness, she prayed when she felt she had no options left.

And there, in the parking lot of a Chinese restaurant, on a clear, cold, snowless February day in 2003, she heard something. She heard four simple words. It wasn't a voice, but a distinct thought.

"Go climb that mountain."

Sheryl looked up and there, in front of her was one of the largest and most majestic mountains around. She knew immediately that Mount Olympus was her mountain. There was only one trailhead in the area that Sheryl knew about, and it just so happened to be on Mount Olympus. It wasn't too far from her home, so she was slightly familiar with it.

Without waiting another moment, Sheryl drove straight there and broke just about every rule in the Bible of hiking. She didn't tell anyone where she was going. She didn't have sturdy boots. She didn't have any food or water. And she was alone.

But armed merely with determination and a will to "go climb that mountain," she started up the trail. This was not a stroll up a hillside. The trail was steep, rugged, and challenging. Sheryl was in no shape, physically or emotionally, to be out on the mountainside. But her heart was more persuasive than her head.

"I decided to start hiking until I could hike no more, until I had more pain in my legs than I did in my heart." It was fortuitous for her that she hadn't exercised regularly in a while, so "it didn't take long for me to hit my limit on the mountain. After less than a mile I couldn't go any more. I headed back down the trail and could barely lift my legs to get in the car. I was SO sore but it felt SO good."

With every step she had taken on that trail, she felt she had been able to leave a heavy dose of negative energy. So while she struggled to lift her legs into her car, a large burden had been left on the side of Mt. Olympus. She felt so relieved; she knew she had to do it again. A week or so later, she attacked the mountain again, leaving more of her frustrations on the trail. She hiked twice more in March, each time feeling more liberated and alive than the time before.

There was something about being on the mountain, about tackling this giant rock monster. She could overcome it; she could beat it. She was bigger than the mountain. And every time she climbed it, she felt more invigorated than before. She had discovered this new exploding passion merely by trying to rid herself of depression and frustration. While it was doing wonders for her psyche, she knew it wasn't the best practice to go hiking alone. She needed someone to go with her, but since she didn't have any close prospects, she turned to an unlikely solution. She decided to become a hiking guide.

With those four hikes under her belt, she signed up to be a hiking guide for the Adult Community Ed summer quarter. She had tossed her passion out to the world to see who would latch on and come along for the ride. Five students did. Her summer with those five students was the start of a new chapter in her life.

It resembled *Bad News Bears* go hiking. Sheryl remembers the one lady who wasn't wearing very good shoes. "She fell and I realized I needed to make sure people wear hiking shoes and not high heels." There was another woman who brought her autistic son who was in his mid-20's. While he was fairly skilled and could hike well, his mother ended up spending most of the time watching over him. And there was Ron. "Ron was a great hiker. I kept wondering why he would pay money to hike with this bunch of misfits. But Ron enjoyed the company and was willing to slow down his pace just to not have to hike alone."

"I really didn't know what I was doing. But I had been a musical theatre major and I just decided to give myself the part of 'hiking guide.' I assigned myself that part, just as if I had been in a play, and I told myself to grow into it. Who cares if I wasn't really that part? I had the confidence to stay a couple steps ahead of the group, and my motto was 'just say what you're going to be, and then just be it.'"

Since then, the passion has been spreading. From that first group of six would-be wanderers, Sheryl has picked up steam. She now has an Outdoor Adventure weekly email that goes out to more than 1200 hikers. She takes hundreds of groups on a variety of day hikes. She teaches Dutch Oven cooking classes. She heads up longer excursions to national parks. Since the discovery of what makes her feel alive, she has taken more than 700 hikes, walked more than 3,000 miles, and hiked nationally and internationally, including the Swiss Alps.

She has started a snowshoeing group, a camping and hiking group, a flat-water kayaking group, a national and international outdoor adventure vacation group, a downhill skiing group, a Dutch oven cooking group, a community garden group, and many more. Through these, she has made thousands of new friends.

One new friend is the young man who started it all. Sheryl made a little change. She gained enough confidence and positive energy in her life, and she actually lost all the hatred and anger she had for Steve. "I not only lost it ALL, but I was able to go WAY beyond that and actually face him and tell him that I forgave him, and that I loved him."

Sheryl now hikes every week. You can always find her somewhere off in the wild. From the first week in January to the last week in December, she's out there somewhere. I know. I've been caught up in the excitement just like the hundreds of others who hiked before me.

It was a bitter cold January when the cold inversion traps dirty, almost palpable air in the valley, while the surrounding canyons and mountains beckon the adventuresome. Sheryl is one of those. She convinced me to grab a pair of snowshoes and follow her. Off we went. We marched across little wooden bridges, crossing over ice-clogged streams. We clomped through knee-deep snowdrifts, heading up a steep mountainside. We stopped at a clearing to gaze out at the view of clear blue skies and snow-draped evergreens.

"Oh, you have to go just a little farther," she would prod. "There is the most amazing cliff up here. It looks so dramatic."

"Oh, but just up around this bend is the most spectacular stream. It was all frozen over just last week. You have to see it." "Oh, you can't turn around until you have seen this view up here just a little higher. You'll have the most fantastic view you can imagine."

It's classic Sheryl. She has found a way to engage her heart with her life. And I am following along because I can't resist the excitement and zeal and energy. She is a new person, all because she "climbed her mountain" and found her passion waiting for her.

14

A Color-Coordinated Reunion

Your permission slip

The Adams Family was having a reunion.

We had drawn straws at the reunion two years earlier and I had gotten the short straw, meaning it was my job to plan it out. So I started a few months before the appointed day, getting things lined up.

I spotted a magnificent mountain retreat home that could be rented out by the night. I put in the reservation. I started doing research on family ancestors who had settled the area and some of their experiences. I lined up activities we could do to tie into that. I paid close attention to our cooking segments on TV to see which ideas could lend themselves to a large family group. I formulated a menu plan.

My wife, during this whole time, seemed to be actively involved in the reunion planning. But while she talked about it, I didn't see her coming up with concrete ideas that helped me in my agenda. One evening when I returned from work, she made her declaration.

"Okay, I have it figured out," she announced.

"What do you have figured out?" I obviously didn't know something had to be figured out.

"It's going to be blue and green."

"What's going to be blue and green?" I was still puzzled.

"The reunion," she blurted out, confused that I wasn't on the exact same page, bewildered that I hadn't been wrestling with that obvious challenge.

"You have a color scheme for the reunion?"

"Of course! You have to have a color scheme! And look at these plates I got today," she begged, procuring a stack of bright blue and spring green paper plates. "They're really popular colors right now and it will be perfect for summer."

Then she pulled out some bulk supplies she had found at a factory warehouse sale. Piles of matching blue and green ribbon were mounded on the table next to the plates.

"But I'm really excited about these," and she pulled out some die cut cardstock forms. I wasn't sure what they were.

"What are they?" I finally had the courage to ask.

"They're little boxes. You fold them up and they are bright blue and green, and then inside you can put a little treat. It's perfect for a little welcome gift. You can put it on their bed each night with a little candy or something inside. Don't you love them?! I LOVE them!"

Inside, I wanted to say, "Are you serious? These are just my siblings and their kids. We're out in the mountains. No one needs a color scheme or matching ribbons and especially a little box with a candy on their bed at night!" That's what I wanted to say.

Instead, I said something along the lines of, "Wow. That's, uh, neat."

A few days later, I was trying to iron out a couple details of the reunion schedule, but all my wife wanted to talk about was the dessert bar. The dessert bar? I didn't know we were having a dessert bar.

"Of course we're having a dessert bar! That's what I'm most excited about. I have to leave the first day's activities a little early so I can get to the house ahead of everyone. When they come into the house, the first thing they are going to see is this spectacular display of candy and treats, all in blue and green. I picked up some blue Hershey's Kisses today, and found some blue striped peppermint sticks. I'm going to make cake shooters and I really want to make those fancy French macaron cookies. They will look great in blue and green. I want to have mini-donuts in blue and green. I'm trying to figure out how to get M&Ms in blue and green, but I'm not sure how to do that except to just pick them out of a big bag."

She went on for a while until I finally interrupted. "You have seriously been spending some time planning this all out?"

"Of course I have." And then with almost a dreamy quality in her voice, "sometimes I lie awake at night in bed for an hour just thinking about it. I can't sleep when I'm planning it out, so I just try to dream up more treats and desserts I can have with it and how I can make it spectacular."

I wanted to rebut what she was doing. I wanted to tell her that she didn't need to do any of that. Open a package of Oreos and toss 'em on the counter and no one will know anything is missing. But I knew better. This wasn't about me or my siblings. It wasn't about nourishment after a day in the sun. It wasn't even about the reunion. It was about her and what keeps her awake at night and causes adrenalin to surge and giver her that tingly, butterfly sensation.

"Hmmm," she smiled and winked at me. "I think it's obviously my passion."

If you want to know where your heart is, look to where your mind goes when it wanders.
Henri Frederic Amiel

For some of us, high school was a little bit of a distraction. Such was the case with one of the most popular regular contributors I've interviewed on TV: Relationship Coach Matt Townsend. Viewers are used to seeing Matt help sort out the communication differences between females and males. Back in high school, Matt was just interested in one half of that equation: females.

At Highland High School, Matt was very social -- too social, in fact. He would have been a shoe-in for elected office, but couldn't qualify since his GPA was below the required minimum 3.0. He was there to have a good time, and impress the girls. "I was on the tennis team since it involved the word 'love' and girls were into that," Matt remembers fondly, almost a quarter century later.

No one in his family had ever been to college. No one had taught him how to study. He came from a broken family and admits he was a bit spoiled as he coasted along with not much thought about what the future held. When an adult leader finally sat him down and explained that he had to go to college, it was a little too late to change the course that had been set. His first and only choice, the University of Utah, rejected him and his meager GPA. With few other options, he turned to the small private Westminster College which was happy to take Matt and his less-than-stellar academic accolades, as long as it was accompanied by a hefty tuition check.

Matt signed up for some of the traditional, basic classes: biology, algebra, and anatomy. But he was able to take one extra class and spotted *Public Speaking* as an option. It spoke to him. He had a hint that he was good at speaking. His few forays into the world had garnered some positive feedback. He had been funny and had enjoyed it. With that tentative backing, he signed up for the course.

He had to give about half a dozen speeches on various topics. With a glint of accomplishment in his eyes, he has no problem ticking off the topics. Favorite Person: Paul Harvey. Health Issue: Smoking and the health problems associated with it. Tragedy: Titanic. "I can still remember it so vividly," he says excitedly.

"While I thought I was good at it, it was still terrifying to get up there. The class gave you feedback and I was nervous. It was a performance and it was a little scary. But at the same time, I liked it. I started getting good grades. I started getting good feedback from the class and I loved it. People were basically saying, 'You can do this.' "

Matt knew he *could*, but wasn't sure if he *should* or *would*. That *Public Speaking* class was his springboard. It had given him confidence and success. It catapulted him forward a couple years where his situation was very different. Stellar GPA. Student at the University of Utah. Married to a wonderful and supportive wife, Mardi, who also just happened to be the daughter of a lawyer where there might have been a hint of expectation that the new son-in-law might also pursue a legal career, or something even loftier.

Matt took some law classes, but would squeeze in a communications course for fun. He took pre-med courses, and would include a communications class when he could. He even worked as an EMT on an ambulance (good training for a future doctor) and would study communications between runs. He loved the communications classes. He wanted to speak. He wanted to teach. He wanted to do what he loved. But it wasn't the smart choice. It was risky. It wasn't as reliable. It was harder to get jobs. It wasn't a respectable job, like lawyer or doctor.

His passion told him to be in one spot. His head told him to be somewhere else.

Unfortunately, universities don't like fence-straddlers like that. With a deadline approaching, Matt had to pick a path. The young newlywed family council was convened with the matter at hand to select the future. Vocally, Matt was weighing the options between pre-med and pre-law. But Mardi finally and fortunately intervened. She walked her big brown eyes across the fake linoleum flooring in that little red brick house kitchen and stared right at Matt. "You need to do communications. That's what you're good at. That's what you love. That's what you need to do."

"Regardless of what I had been saying, that was really what I wanted to hear. With her affirmation, I had been given permission to pursue my passion."

It was the same message that his fellow students in the Westminster public speaking class had told him. Now it was coming from the person who knew him the best and loved him the most, "You can do this." Permission and affirmation rolled into four words.

He volunteered at KUTV, doing anything they would have him do. He progressed to be the Assignment Editor on the weekends. He did the overnight hourly news updates where he claims he bonded with nursing mothers, up late, feeding their babies. "If someone recognized me in the grocery store, I knew she was a new mother." The more he did TV, the more he loved it. "I loved talking to people. I loved communicating with people. I loved relating to people." While he loved the performance part of it, he didn't love the detail part of it. His passion drove him forward to find something else.

He went back to school to get a Master's Degree and started teaching some classes. As part of that, he read the book, "The 7 Habits of Highly Effective People." It spoke to him. So did his wife who was about to give birth to their first child. She wanted to quit working and stay home. Matt's part-time teaching assignment wasn't going to bridge the financial gap. So he turned to Franklin Covey.

Franklin Covey was the company that had put out the whole "7 Habits" program. Since it was Matt's new discovery, he figured it was a logical place to work. He didn't know anyone there. He didn't have a contact or an "in" with the company. "But I just went up and applied 'cold turkey'," he confessed.

Matt's passion was teaching and presenting information. That was exactly what Franklin Covey specialized in. But it wasn't as if they were going to hire some fresh-faced 20-something kid to present their information. The job was in sales. It wasn't what he wanted to do. But it would be a little more financial stability and it was a way in the door.

At Franklin Covey, Matt quickly began plotting how he could do what we really loved to do. It didn't take long before he had dreamed up a scheme. He volunteered to teach the "7 Habits" program to all the new hires. "I came up with this idea. Once a week, on a Thursday or Friday afternoon, I would give up my lunch hour and teach all the new employees my own course on the '7 Habits'. It let me pursue my passion of teaching and presenting."

It also got him in front of all the new employees coming through the doors.

Not long after, Franklin Covey brought in a new executive recruiter. It was the job of Todd Davis to track down the best talent available to teach the Franklin Covey programs to corporations around the world. Todd had an eye for people who have a passion for teaching and presenting.

Since Todd was technically a new employee, he was told about this course that one of the employees in sales had worked up. It was an overview of the "7 Habits" and would be great for him to take. It was a lunch hour class that Todd might find helpful.

And that's exactly how Executive Recruiter Todd Davis found himself on a Thursday afternoon sitting in a class being taught by Matt Townsend who was trading his lunch hour for a little passion fuel.

"He loved it…loved it," Matt gives a little emphasis to the second half of the sentence. "He thought it was the coolest thing. And he told me to try out to be a presenter. The only problem was that they weren't hiring a presenter just then. So I decided to do some other things while I was waiting."

Matt left his sales job and went to work with various Franklin Covey authors developing content. He went out to high schools to teach leadership courses. He honed his skills. He developed his style. He kept teaching his lunch hour classes.

Then came the announcement Matt had been waiting for. Franklin Covey was launching a search for a new facilitator/presenter. Todd came to Matt personally and encouraged him to apply. But Matt wouldn't be the only candidate to toss his hat in the ring.

Applications came pouring in from around the country. In the world of "presenting" this was one of the most coveted positions around. Picture Matt Lauer stepping down and an ad being posted for his position. Picture Martha Stewart needing someone to take over for her. Picture Bill Gates searching for someone to take his reins. This was big.

Out of the 100+ applications, every single one of them had more experience than Matt. Every single one of them had better credentials than Matt. Every single one was older than Matt. "I was only 26 years old!" Matt is quick to point out. "I don't know what I was thinking. They were all 10-20 years older than I was, so they were much more experienced."

The field was narrowed down to the top ten. Matt made the first cut. It might have been a professional courtesy from Matt's mentor Todd, but either way, Matt was still in the running. The ten were all bought in for two days of a selection process. The first day was interviews; the second day was live presentations. "They were all older and richer. They had their two-thousand dollar suits and their two-hundred dollar ties. They were looking good and smelling good," Matt sniffs.

"On the first day, they sat around and tried to intimidate me. It worked. They were so polished and there I was, this young 26-year old kid. But this is what I really wanted to do. It was my passion."

Matt went home after Day 1. He was a wreck. He kept rehearsing in his mind what he had to do the next day. The more he thought, the sicker he felt. "I was so anxious it felt like my stomach was in knots. I was so nervous. I kept thinking about what was up the following day. Even though I kept going over my presentation, I was still really nervous.

"This was everything I had ever wanted to do. It was all I wanted to be. This was my dream."

Looking to calm his soul, Matt grabbed the Bible and just flipped it open. Serendipity and providence smiled as the book fell open to the fourth chapter of 1 Timothy.

"Let no man despise thy youth," the words came at Matt with both force and peace. "But be thou an example...Neglect not the gift that is in thee."

The words filled his soul and lifted him up with confidence and calmness. They spoke to him and allowed him to live his passion. Just as he had received permission from his fellow students at Westminster, just as he had received permission from his wife Mardi in their small kitchen, he now felt that same permission from an even higher source.

The next day, armed with his recently acquired permission, he marched into the presentation room. "I went in there with my 12 dollar tie and my 'buy one, get the second for just a dollar' suit, and the whole time I was thinking that no one can be more passionate about this than I am. I just had to do what I loved and what I knew I was good at."

After each of the ten, the search committee had a quick pow-wow to discuss the person. After Matt's presentation, the discussion went much longer. "Are you really going to be able to hire a 26-year old? Are we really going to be able to sell his services to big clients and important corporations? Is he really going to work with the image we are selling?" The debate went on for quite some time.

After all ten had finished their presentations, the committee met to make their final decision. While the ten sat, cloistered together in a waiting room, the committee summoned them, one by one, to join them in a conference room. While the candidates entered by one door, they exited a completely different door, so the remaining hopefuls never had any idea who had been selected and who had been dismissed.

As each of the ten was called in, Matt's heart sank. He knew his hopes were slowly slipping away since he hadn't been asked in. He felt sick again. He felt nervous again. He tried to boost his spirits by convincing himself this had been a good experience and he was in a better position for the next opportunity, when he was older and more experienced. Maybe that would be his · chance.

In the meantime, six of the candidates had been invited in, and had mysteriously disappeared. Finally the entire search committee joined the last four candidates in their waiting room. They announced that they could just meet with all four of the remaining candidates at the same time. "I knew that was a bad sign," Matt remembered.

"We have met with a lot of really great people," one of them announced. "And everyone really did a great job. There were just a few who did a little better than the rest." Then there was a pause. It was long enough to make Matt feel even sicker.

Then it came. "And you're our four! Welcome to the team!"

And with that announcement, Matt became the youngest trainer at Franklin Covey. He got the green light to do what he loved. He got to do what he knew he was good at. He had been given permission at each step along the way. He knew others were supporting him and he could be successful, which, by the way, he was.

DARIN-ISM NO. 14

Don't stand in the way of your own future. Discover what your passions are, then plot a plan of pursuit.

So who needs to give you permission? If it's someone else, just smile, wink, and confess, "I guess it's just my passion." Then just do what makes you happy.

If it's you, take inspiration from the many who have found their passions and also found something more. They have found answers to their challenges. They have found motivation. They have found careers. They have found power. They have found success. They have found life.

Don't stand in the way of your own future. Discover what your passions are, and then plot a plan of pursuit. And if you need to, just look yourself in the mirror, smile, wink, and confess, "I think it's obviously my passion."

About the Author

Darin Adams has plenty of passions. The list has grown as he has crisscrossed the country for more than 30 years working at TV stations.

- Salt Lake City, Utah: Psych (TV)
- Louisville, Kentucky: The Kentucky Derby
- Boston, Massachusetts: New England Patriots
- Peoria, Illinois: Minor league baseball games
- Pocatello, Idaho: Ping Pong
- Lewiston, Idaho: Waffles
- Kalispell, Montana: Pasta

He is always passionate for a family game night with his wife and four kids. You can often find him playing croquet in the backyard or going on walks or hikes near his home in Fruit Heights at the foot of the Wasatch Mountains in Utah.

He is always anxious to share his passions with others, as long as it doesn't involve him actually sharing his Nutella or fry sauce. He has spoken to and helped thousands of people discover and engage their passions. You can contact him at darinspeaks.com.